D0417565

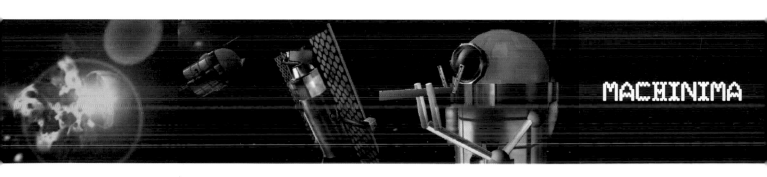

MACHINIMA

MACHINIMA

MATT KELLAND, DAVE MORRIS, AND DAVE LLOYD

ILEX

MACHINIMA
Copyright © 2005 The Ilex Press Limited

First published in the United Kingdom in 2005 by
I L E X
3 St Andrews Place
Lewes
East Sussex
BN7 1UP

I L E X is an imprint of The Ilex Press Ltd
Visit us on the Web at:
www.ilex-press.com

This book was conceived by:
I L E X, Cambridge, England
Publisher: Alastair Campbell
Executive Publisher: Sophie Collins
Creative Director: Peter Bridgewater
Managing Editor: Tom Mugridge
Project Editor: Ben Renow-Clarke
Design Manager: Tony Seddon
Designer: Jonathan Raimes
Junior Designer: Jane Waterhouse

British Library Cataloguing-in-Publication Data.
A catalogue record for this book is available from
the British Library.

ISBN 1-904705-64-2

Printed and bound in China

For more information on this title please visit:
www.web-linked.com/machuk

CONTENTS

INTRODUCTION

6

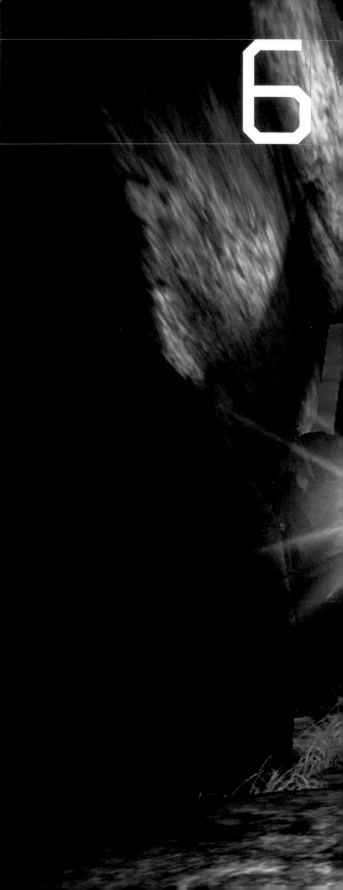

Many of us dream of making movies. Sadly, few of us ever realize that dream. The sheer cost of making a movie is such that only the most talented, the most dedicated, and the most fortunate are entrusted with the task of creating the most exciting of modern art forms. The rest of us have to watch and keep dreaming.

Machinima promises to change that. Piggybacking on the breakneck pace of development of computer game technology, it puts the resources required to make exciting movies into the hands of literally millions of people worldwide. With far greater potential than the simple video camera, it can bring an entire film studio into the home, complete with sets, actors, and special effects.

For aspiring film-makers the world over, machinima is nothing less than a dream come true.

'**Machinima is maturing so rapidly, some predict it will soon be a major force in animation, especially with the imminent arrival of a new generation of hardware and software promising an era of photo-realistic** *cinematic computing*.'
LEANDER KAHNEY, *Wired*

'**Machinima is emerging as a genuine new art and entertainment form.**'
MARK DONALD, *PC Gamer*

Bot (2004), by Digital Yolk, shows that machinima can be as beautiful as any other medium.

WHAT IS MACHINIMA?

THE SHAPE OF THINGS TO COME

Machinima heralds the film-making medium of the future. What started out with a few game fans recording footage of their game alter egos messing around has now become the most exciting new way to make films. Unbelievable, yes, but who'd have thought that William Henry Fox Talbot taking a picture of his bedroom window in Wiltshire, England, would one day lead to Hollywood and *Star Wars*?

From humble beginnings less than a decade ago, machinima is making its presence felt in mainstream animation, music video, and television, and has even penetrated Hollywood itself. In its way, machinima is as revolutionary as the birth of computer graphics, which have changed the way films are made.

Before we show you how to make machinima, we're going to take you on a whistlestop tour of where it all began, who's doing it, and what exactly it is they're doing.

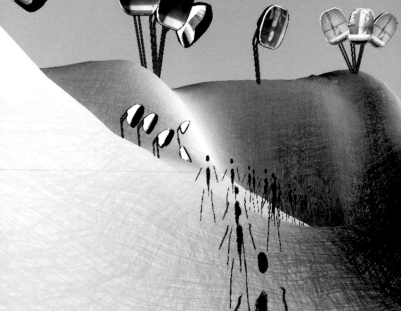

*Machinima comes in many forms, sometimes with barely a trace of its evolution from games. **Scrap** (2004, FAR RIGHT), by Folklore Studios, and **The Journey** (2004, CENTRE RIGHT), by Friedrich 'Fiezi' Kirschner, were both made in Epic's **Unreal Tournament 2004**. Julien Vanhoenacker's disturbing **Anthem** (2003, ABOVE) was created in a custom 3D engine.*

PART 1

'The bottom line is the bottom line: compared to a computer-generated animated film like the critically acclaimed *Toy Story* or the box-office bomb *Final Fantasy*, it costs next to nothing to produce a full-length machinima feature.'

Matthew Mirapaul, *The New York Times*

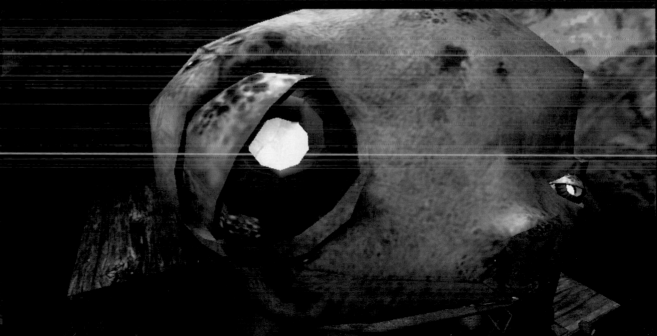

MAKING FILMS IN A VIRTUAL 3D WORLD

10

Machinima is *the art of making animated films within a realtime virtual 3D environment*. Or, to put it in simpler terms, machinima means making films out of games. And, confusingly, the word is often also used to describe both the actual films made this way, either individually or collectively, and the process by which they were made.

So *Red vs Blue* is a machinima, and *Anna* was made in machinima. Logically, we might think that one should be called 'a machinimated movie' and the other 'the process of machinimation'. Don't worry – it's no more confusing than using the term 'film' to describe the movie *Apocalypse Now*, the photographic stock on which it was shot, and what Francis Ford Coppola actually did to create it. By the end of this book, you'll happily be using all three senses of 'machinima' interchangeably without noticing.

So what's machinima all about? Let's go back to that opening sentence. It's about making animated films in a new and different way, and it's about using 3D game engines to do more than just playing games.

Traditional 3D animation, if something barely two decades old can be called 'traditional', is slow and laborious to create. Every part of every shot has to be set up by hand – cameras, lights, characters, expressions, movements, special effects – and then rendered into a film before the animators can see what they're getting.

Machinima makes the process much faster. Everything happens right in front of your eyes, just as it does when you're playing a game or filming a live-action film. You want to see the hero run up the stairs while being chased by bad guys firing machine guns, onto the roof of a blazing office building, and leap off the parapet just as it explodes? Of course you do; action makes for great films. It's the kind of sequence that's expensive in traditional animation because of the complexity of the animation, and even worse in live action because of all the special effects and stuntmen you'd need. But it's the staple fare of many modern games; you've probably played games like it. It's only a very short step from playing the scene in a game to turning it into an exciting machinima movie. In the rest of the book, we're going to show you how it's done.

'Machinima is the convergence of film-making, animation, and game development.'

PAUL MARINO, *Executive Director,*
Academy of Machinima Arts & Sciences

Most machinima is very recognizably derived from games. **Ours Again** (2004, ABOVE), from Mu Productions, and **A Hard Road** (2004, ABOVE RIGHT), by Ian 'Pappy Boyington' Kristensen, were both built in **Battlefield 1942**, developed by Digital Illusions. Rooster Teeth has enjoyed huge success with **Red vs Blue** (2003–4, RIGHT), developed from Microsoft's **Halo**. Steve Twist's **The Bank Job** (2004, BELOW) uses characters from **Unreal Tournament 2004**.

MACHINIMA AND GAMES

'Every time we see a machinima film based on one of
our games, it makes us very proud to see the effort and
love put into these movies, and that someone chose
our work as a basis for creating theirs.'

JOHAN PERSSON, *Creative Director, Digital Illusions*

To understand machinima, you first need to understand videogames. Strictly speaking, you don't need to use an actual game engine to make machinima. Any piece of software that can create and run a 3D world in realtime will do. But since almost every one of those around at the moment was originally designed and built as a game engine, a brief digression into the world of videogames is called for.

The incredibly rapid pace of development of 3D technology was driven partly by the animation industry, partly by the CAD (computer-aided design) industry, but mostly by the games industry. Ten years ago, most games only had two dimensions. Sometimes they made an attempt to introduce perspective or place objects in the foreground to create the illusion of depth, but generally they were flat. The player could only see the world from certain angles; moving the viewpoint would destroy the illusion.

Since the mid-1990s, 3D games have become the norm for PCs and game consoles. Even cell phones are becoming capable of running 3D games. Early games used simpler 2D characters called 'sprites' in environments that could handle up and down, but not over and under, like a high-tech Pollock's theatre. But as computer power advanced, the worlds of games became increasingly sophisticated; characters became fully animated, the sets became highly detailed and realistic, and game developers included elements of simulation into their visual models. The game world became a stage on which players could act, and an environment with which they could interact.

Modern videogames demonstrate unprecedented levels of realism, with detailed sets, shadows, lighting, high-quality facial models, and fully interactive environments.
LEFT ABOVE: **Lord of the Rings: Third Age** *(2004), by Electronic Arts.*
RIGHT: **Fable** *(2004), by Big Blue Box.*
LEFT AND BELOW: **Halo 2** *(2004), by Bungie.*
BELOW RIGHT: **Half-Life 2** *(2004), by Valve.*

WHAT DOES A GAME ENGINE DO?

THE GAME ENGINE IS THE CORE PIECE OF SOFTWARE THAT MAKES A GAME RUN

The first thing that it does is to create the virtual game world on your screen. All the buildings, furniture, trees, and even the sea and sky are created geometrically in the game engine. This isn't just a static 3D model; trees move and sway, radar dishes rotate, and cars roll along busy streets.

Textures are then placed on top of the geometrical outline. These are cunningly created to present an illusion of more geometrical detail than actually exists. A gravel path in the game world is actually a flat, smooth plane, but looks like a bumpy, gritty surface. To save on processing power, the engine usually works at multiple levels of detail. At a distance, the exterior of a temple may simply appear grey, but as you approach, you can make out shapes, which turn out to be ornate carvings. The developer creates different textures for the temple, and the engine selects the texture with the correct level of detail.

Lighting completes the visual illusion. Objects cast shadows, and shiny objects reflect. The colour and intensity of light changes the atmosphere. With the flick of a virtual switch, a friendly town becomes a creepy, deserted haunt for zombies.

Where a game engine differs from other 3D graphics technologies is that it now has to bring this dead world to life.

A game world is peopled with all sorts of characters. Some are controlled by the players. Others, usually called AIs (Artificial Intelligences), are controlled by the game engine. In most games, player characters and AIs are effectively treated identically, except for the aspect of control. They can walk around, run, climb, gesture, open doors, drive vehicles, and, usually in a game, shoot at each other.

Whenever the game engine or a player decides that a character will do something, the game engine plays the appropriate animation and determines the outcome of any interaction with the environment or the other characters. If, for example, the game engine decides that an AI is going to shoot an anti-tank gun at an armoured car, it has to show the animation of the AI selecting the weapon, aiming it, and firing it. It then determines where the shell hits, and then the effects of it hitting. This could create a chain of events: the armoured car explodes and is hurled into the air, killing the occupants and crushing a poor infantryman who happens to be underneath it when it lands.

Interactions like this are controlled by a component called the physics engine. The physics engine defines the physical properties of objects in the game world: whether they bounce, break, or bend. When a bullet strikes a pane of glass, it smashes. When a car takes a bend too fast, it skids or rolls.

Interactions also trigger the sound module within the game engine. This controls ambient sounds, such as wind, rain, or waterfalls, as well as event-driven sounds such as gunshots, shouts, or footsteps. The sound module not only plays the correct sound, but also modifies it so that it appears to be coming from the correct place in the stereo or surround mix.

In effect, a game engine creates an entire, if simplified, virtual world. Machinima is the art of making movies in that virtual world.

Below: **Khan** *(2004), a Korean MMORPG from Mirinae.*
Below right and centre: **Herrcot** *(2004), by Naontech of Korea.*
Right: **World of Warcraft** *(2004), by Blizzard.*
Far left: **Far Cry Instincts** *(2005), by Crytek.*

GAME MODS

As long as there have been videogames, people have made their own modifications (mods) to them, with or without the support of the game developers. Back in the days of *Doom*, gamers quickly got bored with the basic game. Once players knew all the hiding places and all the enemies, the challenge went out of the game. Enterprising players found ways to create their own levels (game worlds), and their own skins (characters). *Quake* clans frequently created their own skins as their clan uniform.

Other mods made changes to the game itself, such as altering the range of a weapon, or how fast characters could move, or how high they could jump. While these types of mods were regarded as cheating by many players, they demonstrate how far the modders would go in changing the capabilities of the game engine.

Today, many games are designed to be modded, and the developers themselves create and support the mod tools. *Battlefield 1942*, as the name suggests, was originally a World War II game. Modders created versions set in the Gulf War,

World War I, *Star Wars*, involving pirates in the Caribbean, spaceship combat, and a *Mad Max* post-holocaust world. *Unreal Tournament 2004* is probably the most modded game of all. Originally a fairly standard science-fiction shoot-'em-up like *Quake* or *Halo*, its many mods include *Air Buccaneers*, a steampunk variant where players control armoured zeppelins, and attempt to blast each other out of the sky, and another set in the twilight days of Atlantis. Epic, the creators of *UT2004*, run regular competitions for the best mod.

For machinimators (film-makers using machinima), modding is a vital piece of the puzzle. It doesn't matter if the story is set in a world that doesn't currently exist in a commercial game, or if the basic game doesn't have exactly the right characters. As long as the engine does all that the machinimator wants it to, sets and characters can be added. There's nothing stopping machinimators from recreating medieval Prague in *Unreal Tournament*, or an Antarctic research station in *Battlefield*. *Half-Life* could play host to Al Capone or the Stainless Steel Rat – or both.

'Epic [Games] is very interested in seeing a thriving mod community. Not only does it extend the life of the base product, keeping it installed and moving new units, but the mod community is also a great recruiting resource for our own company, as well as those who license Epic technology.'

'The spread and the quality is what amazes me the
most. There are mods that excel with all their detail,
their realism, their craziness and most of all their
fantasy of what the *Battlefield* engine can turn into.'

LARS GUSTAVSSON, *Producer, Battlefield 2, Digital Illusions*

FAR LEFT: Games such as **Unreal
Tournament 2004** *and* **Battlefield 2**
(2005) are designed to be modded.
LEFT: Trauma Studios' **Battlefield 1942
Desert Combat** *(2003) used the World
War II game to create a modern era
combat game.*
RIGHT: The **Dead Cities** *mod for* **BF1942**
moves the game into a post-holocaust
Mad Max *world.*
BELOW: Ian Kristensen's **Dead Cities** *(2004)
machinima was a trailer for the mod.*
Air Buccaneers *(2004) is a steampunk
variant of* **Unreal Tournament 2004.**

MACHINIMA VS CONVENTIONAL 3D ANIMATION

The end product of machinima is the same as the end product of any other form of 3D animation: a 3D animated film. So what's the difference between creating a movie in machinima and conventional 3D animation using CGI software such as *Lightwave* or *3D Studio Max*?

'It's a production choice really. There is no right or wrong, better or worse. It's all a matter of creative expression and the tools and methods you wish to use. Many consider machinima for many reasons, from the low cost of entry, to the benefits of a kick start in production based on using included game content, to the enjoyment of working on the cutting edge of realtime 3D graphics.'

KEN THAIN, *Machinimator*

The versatility of machinima:
Scrap (2004, BELOW), by Folklore
Studios, is a gentle fantasy,
while **Maxim of Many, Credence
of One** (2004, BOTTOM) from
Sturmgrenadier OGS, is a hard-
edged futuristic war story.

When you film in machinima, you are filming in a virtual world. True, it's still only made of electrons and phosphor glows, but this virtual world has a sense of reality about it. It has gravity, so if you leave something in mid-air, it will fall down, accelerating until it lands on something (and then maybe break or bounce when it gets there). Objects have solidity and mass to them. Drive into a wall, and the car crashes. Throw a barrel

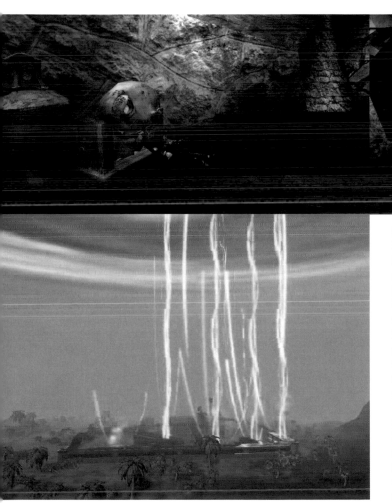

at a character, and he will get knocked back. Fire a rocket at him, and he'll die. The inhabitants of this virtual world may have intelligence and behave semi-autonomously: give them a cake and they'll thank you before eating it. Stand near a lift and tell them to summon it, and with one click of a mouse, they'll figure out that they have to turn towards it, press the button, wait for the doors to open, and get into it. Trees and grass wave in the virtual wind, and water ripples and shimmers when you step in it. Objects create sounds automatically – a door opened offscreen onto a busy street will allow that hint of street noise to filter in from the appropriate place, its ambience modified by the room the camera is in.

The traditional animator, on the other hand, works in a world that only exists visually. Everything that makes the world behave in a real way has to be put in by hand, or it will remain static in perpetuity. An object placed in mid-air will stay there unless made to fall, and will fall right through the floor unless made to stop. Everything that happens does so because the animator consciously made it happen – the character had to be made to turn, his hand stretched out to the button, the button depressed and lit up, the doors opened, the character made to turn and step in, and the doors closed again. And every sound has to be created and mixed in individually.

MACHINIMA VS CONVENTIONAL 3D ANIMATION

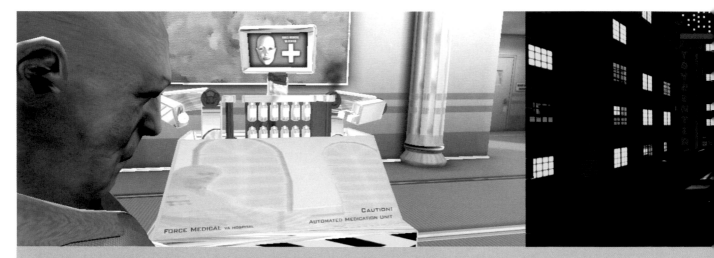

The machinimator has at his disposal a library of animations that he can call on, and can then control his characters like a virtual puppeteer. Simple keyboard controls and mouse clicks tell the character what to do, and the game engine then works out how to show it on the screen without human intervention. The machinimator doesn't have to think about keyframes, worry about footslip, inbetweening, or any of the things that preoccupy real animators. In other words, machinima makes the simple things so easy that the film-maker doesn't have to think about them, and can concentrate on the film itself.

However, simplicity comes at a price. Compared to more expensive forms of animation, particularly at the level of *Shrek* or *Finding Nemo*, machinima characters seem lifeless and unexpressive. The traditional animator has control over every frame of film, every bone in the skeleton, and every fold of cloth. He can create a picture-perfect animation, where every little gesture and nuance is precisely controlled.

The machinimator is limited to what the game engine can do and the animations in his library. Just as Gerry Anderson's *Thunderbirds* puppets could not easily smile, walk through doors or pick up objects, most machinima characters cannot easily cry, hug each other, or even sit down. But despite their simplicity, even for the time, Anderson managed to tell exciting stories with interesting characters that are still popular four decades later. The skill in creating machinima is to work within the constraints, and use a combination of technical and creative solutions to work around them.

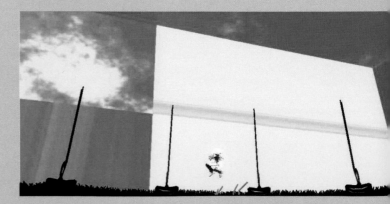

Sparked Memory (2004, ABOVE), by Cswat, and *The Tournament* (2003, BELOW), by Friedrich Kirschner, push the **Unreal Tournament** engine to its limits in the range of visual styles they employ, including full 3D animation, flat animation, motion blur, and mixed media.

'I am fascinated at how the ability to edit captured action at the level of events and objects in the 3D world, rather than at the lower level of conventional linear frame-by-flattened-2D-frame editing of video, would allow for new kinds of mix-based compositional creative approaches to film.'

ANTHONY BAILEY, *Machinimator*

MACHINIMA VS LIVE ACTION

It's not just animators who see machinima as an alternative way of working. Machinima allows film-makers to do things that they couldn't do in a live action film without huge budgets. 'Making an action movie with guns, explosions, and special effects with virtually no money was enticing – *Only the Strong Survive* cost zero dollars to make!' says machinimator Jason Choi.

As with any other form of animation, machinima frees the film-maker from many of the constraints of the real world. This is immediately obvious when it comes to set building and locations. Building fabulous science fiction, fantastic, or historical sets is no more complex or expensive than a street or shopping mall. The entire cast and crew can be transported from the icy wastes of the Yukon to the sun-racked Gobi Desert or to a submarine in the Marianas Trench in seconds. Locations like these, and hence stories based on them, are practically impossible for any but the biggest films. Although the BBC could get away with creating alien cities out of plywood or gravel pits for *Doctor Who* 20 years ago and more, audiences today expect better. Low budget film-makers can create far more convincing sets digitally than they can in reality.

Special effects are also cheap and easy by comparison. In the virtual world, you can blow up the same building or car over and over again. There's no pressure to get the shot

exactly right the first time – everything can always be reset and reshot, and no damage is done. And as if that weren't enough, it's possible to change the world. You could, for example, temporarily reduce gravity to make characters jump higher or further, or invert the set to easily allow characters to run across the ceiling. Stuntmen can be shot, hurled from ludicrously high precipices, thrown through windows, and run over by 18-wheelers without a word of complaint or intervention by the insurance company – and they'll get up and do it over and again until the director is completely happy with their performance.

Unlike traditional animation, machinima maintains that feeling of live anything-can-happen action that directors – in film, but particularly in television – enjoy. Instead of having to plot every single shot, every minute gesture, and every careful camera movement in advance, the machinima director is working in a live environment. By working with a cast of real people, albeit in a virtual world, the director can improvise, shooting fast and choosing shots as if on a real location. Looking through the virtual camera is exactly like looking through the lens while on set. Actors deliver a performance to camera, which they can immediately review and retake until it works.

CAMERA A3   29/09/2

Films like these would require
huge budgets to film in live action.
Machinima brings them within the
grasp of the home movie-maker.
The Bank Job (2004, BELOW LEFT), by
Steven Twist. **The Everseason** (2004,
BELOW) by Ken Thain. **The Hero** (2002,
RIGHT) by The Northern Brigade.

'It is such an ordeal to get a film made – that's one
reason why machinima is such a great opportunity.
As a production manager, to whom logistics is the
name of the game, I suffered many pains from finance
to location permits in urban intersections and so on.
Making machinima is dreamy by comparison.'

INGRID 'COYOTE REPUBLIC' MOON, *Film-maker and Machinimator*

MACHINIMA VS PRE-RENDERED SEQUENCES

The biggest difference between machinima and other forms of computer animation is that everything happens in realtime. In a game, the player needs to be able to see the effect of moving around or shooting someone instantly. The game developer cannot predict what the player is going to do, so the game engine has to work out everything as it happens. Characters move around, crouch and shoot at each other, bullet holes appear on the walls, lights flicker on and off, and buildings collapse. In just 1/60th of a second, the game engine has to render everything the player can see – complete with textures, shadows, and reflections – work out what has happened in the game world, and then do it all over again. Filming machinima is as fast as using a camera. You record it as it happens, and immediately the footage is ready for playback.

By contrast, rendering 3D animation is slow and laborious. Once the animator has created the animation sequence, it is then turned into a movie sequence a single frame at a time. Each frame can take minutes or hours to generate, depending on the level of detail required. A simple shot of a character crossing a room can take hours to render. Before he can see the results of the shot, the animator can only wait as the footage is gradually constructed.

The reasons game engines can render so fast is that they trade speed for quality. Traditional 3D graphics tools use complex techniques such as raytracing, which calculate exactly how light scatters from various surfaces, and how that reflected light illuminates other surfaces. Calculating that for a complex scene with many objects made of different materials with different reflective properties, and using many light sources of different intensities and colours, is a highly computationally demanding task. As computer power increases, the sophistication of the light models increases. Traditional animators also use considerably more detailed models than game developers. In *Final Fantasy: The Spirits Within*, Square modelled every hair on Aki's head individually. The highlights on her hair were created by calculating exactly how her hair should lie at any given moment, and how the light would fall on it.

By comparison, game engines cheat. They have comparatively crude lighting algorithms that can be applied fast, and although not strictly accurate, they look more or less right. Models are simple; a character's ponytail may sway as she moves, but it's a simple solid block, not a bundle of hairs. Pause the film and zoom in, and the difference is clear, but when viewers are concentrating on the action, they don't notice.

ATi rhinofx

'Not so long ago, cinematic-quality renderings took hours to complete; with the advent of next-generation game systems, images approaching that quality will be generated at 60 frames per second.'

NICK PORCINO, *Senior Programmer, LucasArts*

Graphics card makers are continually pushing the boundaries of what PCs can render in realtime. **Ruby**, *from ATI, demonstrates incredible quality facial modelling and skin texturing, while their* **Crowd** *demo features literally hundreds of soldiers all moving individually in realtime. NVIDIA's* **Clear Sailing** *demo (ABOVE) features accurate cloth and water modelling, and Timbury's eyes contract and expand according to ambient light levels.*

MACHINIMA VS PRE-RENDERED SEQUENCES

*BELOW AND FAR RIGHT: Promotional pictures from Blizzard's **World of Warcraft** (2004) show the difference between fully rendered images and in-game images. Realtime rendering has a way to go to achieve this painterly quality. However, games such as Big Blue Box's **Fable** (2004, RIGHT), Revolution's **Broken Sword 3** (2003, THIRD RIGHT), and Ubisoft's **Beyond Good and Evil** (2003, SECOND RIGHT) now use machinima techniques to render most of their cut-scenes in realtime, and still achieve quality comparable to television animation.*

CUT-SCENES

Until recently, the gulf between realtime rendering and pre-rendered video was most obvious in games themselves. Many games featured non-interactive video sequences where the player can't do anything, but just has to watch a short film sequence, normally called a cut-scene. Until a few years ago, cut-scenes were always pre-rendered using standard CG animation techniques, because it was the only way to achieve the required visual quality.

Pre-rendering has three disadvantages. The film sequences take up a lot of space on the discs, hence all those games that came on several CDs. Secondly, pre-rendering can create a huge disparity between the visual quality of the cut-scene, and the visual quality of the games. This looks odd and can ruin the suspension of disbelief the game has carefully built up. And lastly, the cut-scenes have to be fixed in advance, which can create continuity errors. Suppose that the hero of the game can choose between several different sorts of hat: a big floppy swashbuckler's hat, a beret, or a cloth cap. If the cut-scene has him in the beret, and the players have him wearing the cloth cap, they will feel momentarily disoriented and it can spoil their enjoyment of the game.

By using machinima, cut-scenes are generated in realtime using the same game engine that runs the game. This massively reduces the data requirement of the cut-scenes, so the developer can fill the CD with music, art, and game code instead of video. The quality is identical, even down to using exactly the same sound and video settings that the player has selected for the game, and all the continuity is preserved. In some games, the player can even continue to move the camera around and have limited control over the character during a cut-scene, and the game engine will continue to play out the scene.

THE NEXT GENERATION

As computers continue to become more powerful, it's worth reflecting on the fact that the average home PC running a game engine can now render in realtime what only a top-end graphics system could render offline ten years ago. And there's no sign of a slowdown. The newest graphics cards from NVIDIA and ATI, combined with the latest chips for the PC or Mac, and increasingly complex game engines, continue to push the boundaries of what is possible in a virtual world. We will see the world distorted through the transparency of a fairy's wings, booted feet reflected in the sheen of rain glistening on a wet pavement, and the pupils in a character's eyes glint and contract as he steps myopically out into the light.

'Let's say Oddworld wanted to do a 90-minute, direct-to-DVD movie. If we wanted to do it with pre-rendered CG, we'd probably be looking at a $30 million-dollar budget, even with very aggressive economics. If instead we went the machinima route, and ported it to the PC and took advantage of 2MB RAM for texture mapping instead of 64MB, then we could do 90 minutes for $6 million. And what would come out of that would be far more epic than anyone would expect. We could generate enough quality for HD.'

LORNE LANNING, *President, Oddworld Inhabitants*

HISTORY OF MACHINIMA

THE EARLIEST DAYS

'As short and simple as the movie appears to us today, *Diary of a Camper* **established a filmic genre known as machinima.'**

KATIE SALEN, *Interactive Designer and Writer*

Machinima is older than you might at first think. Ever since there have been 3D games, people have been using them to make simple movies. Back in 1994, Id Software's *Doom* allowed players to record game sessions and play them back later in 'demo mode' to show their friends. Driving games such as Microsoft's *Monster Truck Madness* incorporated a replay feature that allowed you to watch the race you'd just finished, viewing it from different camera angles, and cutting between them at will.

With the launch in 1996 of *Quake*, also from Id, things really took off. Multiplayer games of *Quake* became wildly popular. Many players took it up more or less as a sport and formed regular teams, known as 'clans'. The clans used the demo features in *Quake* to show off their prowess. Matches between rival clans were recorded, and *Quake* players from all over the world would watch them with the same intensity as football matches, just for entertainment, or to study the form of their potential opponents. One of the most famous series of demos was *Quake Done Quick*, which showed players getting through

Quake levels at very high speed, collecting all the hidden bonuses and killing all the monsters. For *Quake* fans, this was a masterclass in how to play.

It was a *Quake* clan called the Rangers who created the first true machinima, *Diary of a Camper*. This was a simple story about a lone soldier challenging the clan. By Hollywood standards it wasn't much of a story, but it marked the transition from sports footage to true film-making. The players were choreographed like actors, working to a script, and delivering their lines as plain text, and using one player as a camera.

Diary of a Camper spawned a host of other '*Quake* movies' as they were then known. Film-makers started developing tools such as *LMPC* (Little Movie Processing Center) that allowed them to move beyond the limitations of the basic in-game demo mode. The tool *Keygrip* introduced a technique called 'recamming', which allowed film-makers to add in extra cameras after the footage was initially shot. This freed them from the limitation of the game's first-person viewpoint and allowed them to think in a more film-like way.

'In my DEM (recording format for *Quake 1***) specification document, I wrote: "For people with too much spare time** *Quake* **can replace a full 3D modelling system for cartoons or the like." And somehow it really happened. That's strange.'**

UWE GIRLICH, *Creator of* LMPC

Early machinima: **Diary of a Camper** (1996, LEFT), by the Rangers. **Quake Done Quick** (1997, TOP). **Apartment Huntin'** (1999, ABOVE) and **Hardly Workin'** (2000, RIGHT), by the ILL Clan.

HISTORY OF MACHINIMA 2

THE FIRST MODERN MACHINIMA

30

© Mforma Europe Ltd.

© Mforma Europe Ltd.

January 2000 saw the birth of machinima in its modern form. Hugh Hancock and Anthony Bailey, two of the leading *Quake* film-makers, coined the term by combining 'machine' and 'cinema' to make 'machinema', so that they could include films made with many different games, such as *Unreal Tournament* and *Half-Life*, under a single umbrella. Hancock subsequently misspelled the word as 'machinima' and the new name, with its additional connotations of both 'anime' and 'animation', stuck.

In 2000, Hancock and others launched the website www.machinima.com as a one-stop resource for all machinimators. In June that year, noted US film critic Roger Ebert declared that machinima was an 'extraordinary' new art form.

Early in 2000, Tritin Films released *Quad God*. In many ways it was just another film made in Id's latest game, *Quake 3 Arena*, but with two major differences. For a start, it was 45 minutes long, considerably longer than most of the short films produced up until then. But more importantly, it used a radical new technique, as far as machinimators were concerned. Director Joe Goss captured the footage by recording the on-screen action directly into a video camera. This was then converted into a digital video file and edited on the computer using a standard suite of video-editing software. Tritin released the film as a standalone video, which didn't

require the viewer to watch the film by loading it into *Quake 3*, or even to have a copy of the game. At the same time, over in the UK, pioneering interactive TV game developers nGame were using the same techniques in *Dumb*, a freeware copy of the *Doom* engine, to create their short machinima trailers for *Berlin Assassins* and *Castle Conquerors*.

The immediate reaction of many in the machinima community to *Quad God* took Goss by surprise. Instead of appreciating that machinima could now be enjoyed by people other than game fans, many of them felt that it was wrong to move away from the demo scene, and derided the film for requiring such a comparatively large download. However, *Quad God* enjoyed wide distribution on magazine cover CDs and is now recognized as a key moment in the development of machinima.

Machinima's first commercial venture, Strange Company, was founded back in 1997 in Edinburgh by Hugh Hancock, and it is the only company that works exclusively in machinima production. This was followed in the year 2000 by Katherine Anna Kang, formerly of Id software, who founded Fountainhead Entertainment in Texas. Fountainhead created the first fully featured machinima tool, *Machinimation*, which allows users to create films in *Quake 3*.

Quad God (2000, ABOVE), by Tritin
Films, started the breakout from
the niche of pure '**Quake** films'.
For their Cold War thriller **Berlin
Assassins** (1999, ABOVE LEFT), nGame
recreated 1960s Berlin using **Dumb**.
Fountainhead's **Anna** (2003, RIGHT)
completely broke away from the
game genre.

HISTORY OF MACHINIMA 3

DEMOS AND VIDEOS

The distinction between demos and videos is probably the most important technical aspect of machinima to understand. The key difference between the two formats is that demos are designed to be viewed on a computer within the original game engine, while videos can be watched simply with an appropriate video viewer, either on a computer or on a standard DVD player.

Videos are like films. They consist of a sequence of frames. Each frame contains a complete picture of what the viewer sees. The video viewer then plays those frames at the specified rate to create the illusion of motion.

Demos, on the other hand, don't have frames. Instead, they contain instructions to the game on how to recreate the action. Game instructions are generally very short and simple: use such-and-such a level, bring in this character, walk this way, fire in this direction, change weapon, and so on, and the time at which these occurred. To play the demo, the game engine just executes those instructions as if there were a real person playing the game.

The implications of this are immense. Videos have several major advantages; for a start, anyone can watch them without needing a copy of the game. The machinimator can add in special effects that the game does not support, such as dissolves or film grain. The machinimator also has control over the resolution and level of detail, and the film will look the same wherever it is viewed.

On the other hand, video files are huge. A minute of uncompressed video will take up around a gigabyte. Video files can be compressed significantly, but the video quality can be severely degraded, and it still takes tens of megabytes for even a short film. Demo files are tiny by comparison, and there is no loss of quality. The film plays back on the viewer's machine at the best quality they can run their game. However, if the original game doesn't include all the models and sounds in the film, these additional assets have to be imported and installed. Often the additional assets can be fairly large in themselves, so the complete demo package is as bulky as the video would be.

Demos also allow machinimators to edit films in a unique way. Tools such as *LMPC* or *Machinimation* allow changes directly to the game instructions: for example, altering the time at which a virtual actor moves or fires by changing a line of code in the script instead of having to reshoot the scene from scratch.

Real demo purists, such as Finland's Moppi Productions, create self-contained programs that generate realtime video without the need to install a game engine. This form of demo, though, is increasingly rare.

© Moppi Productions

© Moppi Productions

© Moppi Productions

Halla (2002), by Moppi Productions,
is a hauntingly beautiful, dark
version of the **Little Match Girl**.

© Moppi Productions

HISTORY OF MACHINIMA 4

MACHINIMA TODAY

The last few years have seen an explosion of machinima. As game technology improves and home video-editing software becomes more ubiquitous, more and more people are coming to realize that they can create impressive-looking films at home. And as broadband becomes increasingly common throughout the world, the audience for machinima is growing.

In 2002, leading machinimators including Hancock, Kang, Bailey, and Emmy award-winning animator Paul Marino, of machinima group the ILL Clan, founded the Academy of Machinima Arts & Sciences. Based in Marino's home town of New York, the not-for-profit Academy acts as a central forum for machinimators, promotes machinima to the mainstream animation and film industries, and works with game companies to make game engines and other tools available for use by machinimators. 'Since there is significant added value here for the games companies to realize once the licences are worked out, I'm sure some of them will go for it,' says AMAS co-founder Anthony Bailey.

*Modern machinima is advancing as rapidly as games themselves. **The Tournament** (2003, BOTTOM), by Friedrich Kirschner, is a superb example of what can be done with **Matinee**. **Maxim of Many, Credence of One** (2004, BELOW), by Sturmgrenadier OGS, uses **Planetside** to tell an epic story.*

'Machinima is primitive now, but unlike movies, it is on a technology curve. Next year machinima will be twice as rich, and the year after that traditional movies will look pretty grainy in comparison.'

GABE NEWELL, *Creator of **Half-Life**, Valve Software*

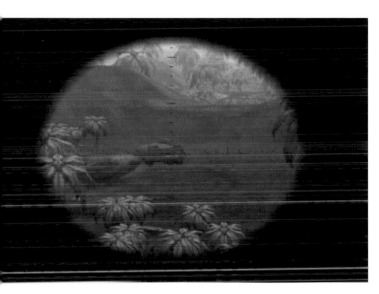

In 2003, the website *3DFilmMaker.com* was set up by animator Ken Thain to promote closer co-operation between traditional 3D animators and machinimators, and *Machinimag*, launched in 2004 by German machinimator Friedrich Kirschner, is the first print magazine devoted to exclusively to machinima.

The release of *Matinee* as part of *Unreal Tournament* marked something of a watershed for machinimators. *Matinee* was originally developed as an inhouse tool to create the ingame cinematics for *Unreal Tournament*. Epic made the decision to make it directly available to the public so that they could create their own films. In combination with Epic's other mod tools for the game, such as *UnrealEd*, *Matinee* creates a platform for creating highly sophisticated machinima, sometimes bearing little resemblance to the original game.

THE MACHINIMA PIONEERS

These individuals are to machinima what Georges Méliès and D.W. Griffith were to film, and what Walt Disney and Ub Iwerks were to animation.

 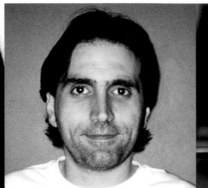 

HUGH HANCOCK is probably the leading figure in machinima today. His Edinburgh-based Strange Company took machinima to new heights in 1999 with its first two films, *Eschaton: Darkening Twilight* and *Eschaton: Nightfall*. Based in the world of H.P. Lovecraft, these films featured original characters and sets, and marked the shift from hobby to professionalism. Hancock founded Machinima.com, the leading resource for machinima film-makers, and together with Paul Marino, Katherine Anna Kang, and Anthony Bailey, founded the Academy of Machinima Arts & Sciences in 2002.

PAUL MARINO of New York's ILL Clan is a leading exponent of machinima as an art form. One of the few current machinimators with experience of mainstream animation, he worked on early machinima comedy classics including *Apartment Huntin'* and *Hardly Workin'*. Marino wrote the first book about machinima, *The Art of Machinima*, published in 2004.

KATHERINE ANNA KANG founded Texas-based Fountainhead Entertainment in 2000. Fountainhead's close relationship with Id Software, where Kang was formerly director of business development, enabled them to work closely with the 3D game experts to produce *Machinimation*, the first fully functional machinima tool suite, as well as several highly rated machinima films, including the award-winning *Anna*.

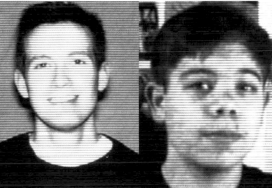

ANTHONY BAILEY was the driving force behind *Quake Done Quick*, one of the leading teams of *Quake* film-makers. He currently develops machinima tools for Strange Company.

UWE GIRLICH was doing his PhD in Germany when he first started looking at how the demo format of Doom and Quake worked. He used this to create *LMPC (Little Movie Processing Center)*, the first machinima tool. He is currently working on a new version of *LMPC*.

ERIC 'STARFURY' BAKUTIS created *Devil's Covenant*, the first feature-length *Quake* movie, back in 1998. Since then, he has worked on a number of other productions, including *The Battle of Xerxes* for Artemis, and *Cancers*. Eric is a leading expert in lip synch tools for machinima and currently works in *Matinee*.

Brothers **JOSEPH** and **JEFF GOSS** head *Tritin Films*, a nine-man outfit based in Pennsylvania. In 2000, they created *Quad God*, the first machinima shot in *Quake 3 Arena*, and the first *Quake* film that didn't require a copy of the actual game to watch. They now produce traditional 3D animation.

KEN THAIN produced the first machinima music video, *Rebel vs Thug*, for hip-hop artist Chuck D. He runs the website 3DFilmMaker.com, and currently works in *Matinee*.

CASE STUDY: *DEVIL'S COVENANT*

38

Devil's Covenant, by Clan Phantasm, was the first full-length *Quake* film, released in 1998. Writer/Director/Producer Eric 'Starfury' Bakutis explains what it was like making films in the early days of machinima.

Like other people playing *Quake*, I was inspired to start making machinima by the Rangers. I had a strong background in sci-fi and fantasy writing and I just thought it was incredibly cool that you could create a film inside a game.

After getting my feet wet with a short film called *The Artifact*, I started on *Devil's Covenant* in early 1997, while still in college. Although I didn't originally intend to create a feature-length film with a two hour, ten minutes running time, I didn't put any limitations on the script.

First, I had to figure out designing levels within the engine, which act as the virtual 'sets'. Then I had to learn how to use some freeware modelling tools to add new 'skins' to the game's models, so that the characters would be unique. Finally, I had to learn a bit of coding (watered down C++) to add special effects and plot-specific functions.

Filming was done using the university computer lab. One or two of my friends in college were on other PCs, networked to the 'camera' PC, where I ran the camera using keyboard and mouse. We also had remote people connect to the server (which we ran in the computer lab after hours) over the Internet.

It was gruelling work for my digital puppeteers. Often, it was as simple as standing in place for 10 or 15 seconds, or, at the most complex, walking a few steps forward, turning left, walking a few steps back, and shooting something. This would go on for hours. For the most part, it was long, tedious, boring work and to this day I have no idea why the people doing it put up with me (although I'm very grateful that they did).

I very quickly learned that it was almost impossible to get three to four people on at the same time due to time constraints, so I added a snippet of code to the engine that allowed me to set up dummies that looked just like the live characters being controlled by the people on the server, but did not require another 'live' PC. I instructed my actors on where to move through in-game chat (a laser pointer-like hack I added to the code of my camera PC assisted in this) and typing 'Action' and 'Cut' at the start of each snippet of scene.

Once I had my raw footage (usually measuring several hours) in the form of *Quake* demo files, I used *Film at 11*, a freeware *Quake* demo editor created by Eric Stern. The editing process was then as simple as deleting all the footage after each 'Cut' but before each 'Action'.

The final step was making the characters speak. For the voices, I put up a post on several *Quake*-related message boards asking people to audition, and was incredibly fortunate to land some terrific voice talent. I added commands to the demo to play the WAV files at set times during the demo's playback. As machinima technology was in its infancy at the time, I didn't bother trying to find a way to make my characters' mouths move. Instead, I relied on the focus of the camera and the audience's rising familiarity with what each character sounded like to signify who was speaking.

I premiered *Devil's Covenant* to an audience of about 80 people at *Quakecon* '98 in Dallas. At the time people hadn't really seen anything of this scope done in the engine. The feedback I got was overwhelmingly positive and very, very rewarding. What really made all the effort worth it for me, however, was knowing that I'd created a story and people had watched it and enjoyed it.

MACHINIMA GENRES

Machinima is as diverse as any other form of film-making. Given a virtual film studio and some actors, people will come up with ever more and more surprising and unexpected ways to use them. And just as with film, television, or animation, machinima is diversifying into several recognizable genres.

Truest to the roots of machinima, there remains a strong strand of fan films that adapt the pure game experience to a non-interactive form. The tradition of showing other players how it's done, which began with *Quake Done Quick* and their ilk, is still alive and well. Most popular among these are the stunt videos (often called skill videos), and films showing hidden parts of the games. Within this, there is an emerging fashion for what could best be called documentaries or reportage.

Comedy is a hugely popular form of machinima. Whether these are original skits, zany visuals set to existing soundtracks, or outrageous parodies, the five-minute sketch is the machinima equivalent of the Web's Flash animations. Often crude, and frequently filled with in-jokes for gamers, they are the starting point for many machinimators.

Where machinima begins to break away from its niche beginnings and starts to challenge other forms of animation is in drama. These are primarily short action films, often based on the worlds of games, but as tools and techniques improve, machinimators are beginning to expand their creative range to encompass a wide variety of stories and settings.

And lastly, machinima has its very own arthouse movement. Some machinimators are pushing the boundaries of what a game engine can do and are producing experimental pieces that seem to bear very little resemblance to their game heritage. Striking, disturbing, and often bewildering, they show that working in machinima has the potential to be as intellectually and aesthetically challenging as any other art form.

*The creative range of machinima is immense. In **Sparked Memory** (2004, ABOVE AND ABOVE LEFT), the viewer is whisked from a realistic world into almost flat cartoons. Perhaps the most frightening thing you could encounter in Blizzard's **World of Warcraft** (2004, RIGHT) is a posse of a dozen orcs all dancing to MC Hammer's **U Can't Touch This**. Video created by JuniorX. Peter Rasmussen's **Killer Robot** (2003, LEFT) takes us to the surface of Mars, and beneath.*

'For every movie there is always something that makes us
go "HOLY &?$# – how did they come up with THAT idea!?"'

JOHAN PERSSON, *Creative Director, Digital Illusions*

INSIDE THE GAME

The more feminine side of gaming is demonstrated by Aktrez (RIGHT) in **Star Wars Galaxies**. Just as in real life, people come to gawp at the chorus lines and their flawless timing. **Star Wars Beauty Pageant** (2004, LEFT AND BELOW), by Aktrez, filmed in **Star Wars Galaxies**.

Halo has been one of the most successful computer games of recent years. It was key to the launch of Microsoft's Xbox console, and it was not long before developers Bungie created a version for the PC. The main website for *Halo*, Halo.Bungie.Org (or HBO, as it's sometimes known), is filled with machinima created by, and unashamedly for, *Halo* fans. Part training video, part game trailer, part bragging features, machinima adds a new way to look at *Halo*. Want to know what happens at the end of the single-player game but not finished it yet? Wondering how to access that high ledge from which your opponents were sniping you in last night's game, or how to climb out of the Blood Gulch gravity well? Or just want to watch some first-class team tactics in action? Download the film.

It's only a short step from demonstrating how the game should be played to showing how to get more out of the game than the designers originally intended. This has given rise to a slew of stunt videos, where gamers demonstrate how to do the most outrageous stunts, with or without game mods. Most action games have their stunt videos, and *Halo* is no exception, but *Battlefield 1942* seems to specialize in them. Many of these films are a true testament to the skills of the performers – if you hadn't seen it done, you'd swear they were cheating. They would certainly make formidable opponents – the Harlem Globetrotters of the *Battlefield* world!

In the world of massively multiplayer online role-playing games (MMORPGs), players join vast virtual worlds, and they can live out an entire alternate life inside them. Although most players (and most games) are usually focused on combat, others enjoy the social life that MMORPGs can give them, and more and more games are giving this aspect more focus. In *Everquest*, two characters got married and organized an extravagant wedding. Powerful sorcerers saved up their spells and laid on a firework show, and high-ranking warriors formed a guard of honour. And of course, there was someone there recording the whole event and making a video of it.

Possibly the most unusual documentary filmed inside a virtual world was *Miss Galaxies 2004*, the beauty pageant – or scholarship contest, as they prefer to call it – that took place inside *Star Wars Galaxies*, complete with swimsuit competition. Aktrez Il'Ustra, the driving force behind organizers Nabooty Entertainment, had experience doing the same thing in real life, and had previously organized contests in *Anarchy Online*. 'The outfits available in the game and the extensive use of emotes (gestures to convey emotion) made it very easy for me to bring what I had learned from competing into the real world,' she says. Enterprising *Galaxies* players made sure they took footage of the event, which was distributed on *PC Gamer*'s cover disc in August 2004.

CASE STUDY: BATTLEFIELD STUNTACULAR

Stunt film *Battlefield Stuntacular* features planes flying upside down under low bridges, jeeps jumping across rivers, spectacular vehicle crashes, pilots jumping from one plane to another in mid-air, and tanks being thrown high into the air while planes loop the loop around them, all to a pumping rock soundtrack. The director, Xanatos, looks back at the production of the film.

In *Battlefield Stuntacular*, we had a crew of between three and seven people in the game at one time, depending on who could actually make it to each filming session. Our biggest sessions didn't work out very well because it's always hard to control all of your actors, and seven was too many. In the background we were using a great program called Teamspeak, in which we could voice chat with each other over the mic instead of relying on typing in *Battlefield 1942*.

The whole filming process took about a week. We were playing day in and day out, literally. Every day we usually started in the evening and ended very late. Of course it took many days before that to get everything planned out before we started filming, and then I had to spend time editing the actual video. The entire process took about two weeks.

I was pleased with the results of some of our footage. We were trying things that seemed impossible to do, but we eventually pulled off most of them! However, there were some stunts we just couldn't manage, and therefore didn't make it into video, unfortunately.

One thing that was particularly irritating was the behaviour of the crew when it came to a big group. There was always someone getting in the way of our plans! For a project like this, it's very hard to get control of everyone when it is such a large group.

There were some things I would have liked to put into the movie, and some things that probably should have been cut from the actual video, but the final product of the movie was, in our opinion at least, quite good.

COMEDY

'An African or a European swallow?'

Monty Python and the Holy Grail

Monty Python's classic film sketches have entertained millions for thirty years and more. They're so popular that they've transcended cult status and become part of Western culture. Unsurprisingly, early machinimators found themselves taking classic comedy soundtracks such as Python and adding visuals taken from games. The Arthurian MMORPG *Dark Age of Camelot* was a natural fit for anything Holy Grail-related.

A Great and Mighty Empire is a long-running comedy series set in the world of *Star Wars*, and created by British outfit UK Mercs. It follows the adventures of two bored Imperial stormtroopers stuck on the Death Star. Witty use of Scottish and Welsh accents add to the absurdity of the situation, as they face tedium, triviality, and grand adventure within the space of a few minutes. Meanwhile, in British Columbia, Ian 'Pappy Boyington' Kristensen produced several comedies set during World War II, most notably *Blabberfield* and *A Hard Road*, which combined elements of stunt films with a witty voiceover.

Machinima has also spawned a host of highly original comedy. In the early days, New York's ILL Clan paved the way with their *Larry & Lenny* series, *Common Sense Cooking with Carl, Apartment Huntin'*, and *Hardly Workin'*. Avatar and Wendigo's surreal *Blahbalicious* set the standard in machinima comedy when it was released in 2002.

As the gaming audience became more widespread, much of the machinima humour became increasingly self-referential. The most successful machinima series of all, with more than 800,000 downloads of each episode, is *Red vs Blue*, set in the world of *Halo*. As its name implies, it deals with the long-running war between the Reds and the Blues, and what life is like for the grunts caught up in the never-ending battle. They muse on the futility of it all – no sooner do they capture the enemy flag than it is magically returned to their base and they have to do it all over again.

At the other end of the comedic spectrum, slapstick is still popular. The machismo and violence innate in most videogames is quickly transformed into comedy by clever editing, a slight adjustment to the frame rate, and the addition of Keystone Kops or Benny Hill music. Adding music to game footage is an easy way to create comedy, as films such as JuniorX's take on MC Hammer's *U Can't Touch This*, performed by orcs in *World of Warcraft*, demonstrate perfectly.

Some comedy is decidedly niche, even for gamers: *The Editor Has You* is about a group of characters inside a game of *Unreal Tournament 2004* hunting down a bunch of players who are cheating by using aimbots, a mod designed to improve the player's aim. The sketch is filled with jokes about creating game maps, and is all but incomprehensible to anyone outside the *UT2004* modding community.

However, not all gaming comedy is targeted solely at fans. Strange Company's pastiche *Tum Raider* was produced for the BBC. 'Lara's away, but her overweight, unfit brother Larry has taken her place....'

LEFT: Danny Coffey's version of **Monty Python and the Holy Grail** (2004). This isn't what developers Mythic Entertainment had in mind when they created **Dark Age of Camelot**.
ABOVE: Strange Company's **Tum Raider** (2003) targets games icon turned silver screen goddess Lara Croft.

CASE STUDY: *RED VS BLUE*

Rooster Teeth's *Halo* comedy *Red vs Blue* is the most popular machinima to date. Now running to some 60 episodes in three series, it has been released on DVD as well as on the Internet. Team member Gus takes us behind the scenes.

The initial idea for *Red vs Blue* came about in the summer of 2002 and we made a trailer for it that August. The project then sat on the back burner until January 2003. We launched the site and released the first episode in early April 2003.

First, we write the scripts a few days before we start filming. Then we distribute the script to the voice actors who record their lines and ad-libs and turn them over to Burnie, the producer. All the audio is then laid down in our editing software (*Adobe Premiere*) and once that's done we start filming video using our Xboxes and try to match it up against the audio. We have four Xboxes networked together. One is dedicated to our cameraman and we can have up to 12 'actors' using the other three Xboxes. Once all the video is filmed, we edit it together and add the letterboxing effect then render the video and distribute it online.

All the tools we use are available off the shelf. We have four Xboxes, thirteen Xbox controllers, a desktop computer with a Canopus video capture card, Adobe Premiere Pro 1.5, Adobe

Audition, and a few Logitech USB microphones. Each episode typically takes 30–40 hours to make.

We typically still use the same hardware and software that we started the series with. We've upgraded to newer versions of the software that have been released since we started, and for season three we started using a new video capture card, but that's about it.

Each week we have about 800,000 video downloads when we are 'in production' and actively releasing episodes.

We have definitely been very surprised about the success of the series. When we started out we figured we'd be happy if we had 3,000 people visit our site each day and we greatly surpassed that number in the first week the series was online.

Initially we decided to release the series on DVD so that we could give them to people who donated to the website and helped support us, then we realized that more people wanted the DVD so we started making more and selling them.

DRAMA

'Can't sing. Can't act. Can dance a little.'

Original screen test report on Fred Astaire.

While comedy and ingame films are primarily the province of the first-time machinimator, most of the committed machinimators are focusing on using the medium for more serious drama. The games heritage of machinima means that it is innately suited to making action films. The challenge for drama creators has been to infuse their characters with the emotion necessary to tell a good story. This has involved developing facial animation tools, lip synch, and custom animations in order to enable game characters to deliver an interesting performance. Although machinima is still a way off from producing its first Anthony Hopkins or Julianne Moore, it's clambering rapidly towards its first Mark Dacascos or Dolph Lundgren.

Most machinima drama is based heavily in the original game world or something visually close to it. Films such as Ken Thain's *Everseason*, Eric Bakutis' *Cancers*, or Oliver Bermes' *The Infiltrators* are all set in a science fiction world straight out of *Unreal Tournament*. *Ours Again*, by Nathan Moller, *ffyr1oett* by Stefan Jönsson and Andreas Lan, and *The River* by Ian 'Pappy Boyington' Kristensen are straight war films generated using the *Battlefield* engine, and Jason Choi's stunning *Only the Strong Survive* is a gangster film unashamedly based on *Max Payne*. In every case, the machinimators have adapted the basic game premise and created a new story. Although the use of sets and models from *UT2004* in *Cancers* is obvious to viewers familiar with the game, there is no presumption that the audience consists of gamers, just as the use of a mansion in a television drama does not assume that the audience at home is interested in the history of architecture. Indeed, to some extent, not being familiar with the game enhances the illusion.

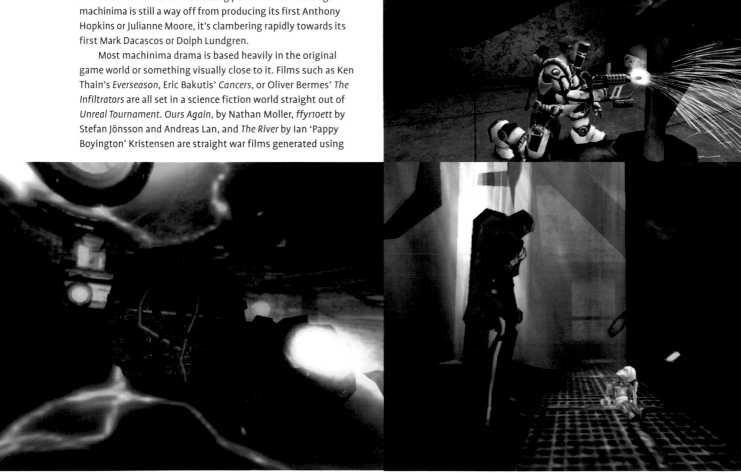

BELOW: **The Infiltrators** (2004)
is a short action piece made
by Oliver Bermes using **Unreal
Tournament 2004**.
BOTTOM: **Anachronox** (2003)
takes the story from a
game and presents it as an
uninterrupted film.

Other dramas use the game world as a starting point and then subvert it. *Bot*, by Digital Yolk, tells the story of a robot in a cyber world who refuses to go out and get shot in a battle, and instead explores his surroundings, looking for something more. *No Licence*, by Short Fuze, used a modified version of *Battlefield 1942* to create a homage to the James Bond films, complete with henchmen in orange jumpsuits and a secret base in a volcano crater. *Haliens* went one stage further and used *Halo* characters to recreate famous scenes from *Aliens*, even using the original soundtrack.

By contrast, *Anachronox* is completely taken from the original Ion Storm game. 'I thought it would be fun to see if I could edit the cut-scenes from the game together in a straight movie narrative', says creator Jake Hughes. 'When the cut-scenes were made, they acted as a bridge between gameplay, so the challenge was how to make the story work. We had to address issues of story flow. Since some of the story happens in game, there were a couple of gaping story holes. Game stories are feeling a lot like movies, especially *Anachronox*. It was conceived that way, written that way, and executed that way... so it all makes sense. I think all story-based games should try to edit together their footage. It's fun, entertaining, and it shows you how to be a better storyteller.'

 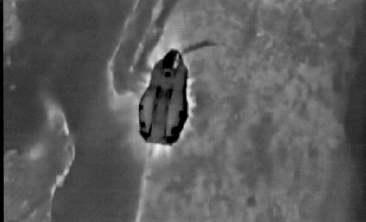

The real frontier for machinimators is the creation of completely original drama that has nothing to do with games, and that stands completely on its own merits. In 1999, Strange Company produced the horror films *Eschaton: Nightfall* and *Eschaton: Darkening Twilight*, filmed in *Quake 2* and set in an eerie Lovecraftian world. More recently, Damien Valentine created *Consanguinity*, an episodic *Buffy*-type story using the *Neverwinter Nights* engine. Although technically crude, the storytelling and camera work draw the viewers in and keep them engaged.

Artemis Software's *The Battle of Xerxes* is almost unique among machinima dramas, being a historical drama with overtones of sword and sandals epics such as *Gladiator*. With clever camera work and good use of flashback, it tells a story of betrayal and vengeance and with no hint of its *Quake 3* roots showing through.

Equally radical is Peter Rasmussen's *Killer Robot*. It is not, as the title suggests, a tale of giant mechanoids rampaging through the streets of Tokyo or Manhattan. Rather, it's a science fiction adventure comedy. It tells the story of Mira, an exploration robot on Mars, who gets bored with rocks, and heads off in search of adventure accompanied by the loyal drone, Sam. Created using *3D Gamestudio* and *Truespace* rather than a conventional games engine, it has a visual style very different to most other machinima. 'I was delighted to see that even with synthesized voices how much of a "performance" was present in the characters. Despite the crudeness of my modelling and my basic animation, the characters have a great deal of personality,' says Rasmussen.

ABOVE: **Haliens** (2002), by ColdVengeance and DemonLite, uses the soundtrack to **Aliens** and replaces the visuals with characters and sets from **Halo**. BELOW: **Gladiator** on a budget: **The Battle of Xerxes** (2003), by Artemis Software.

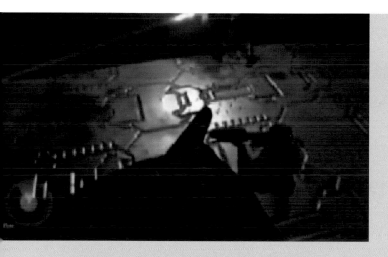

'What makes a good machinima movie are the same things that make a good film in general: story, characters, emotional attachment, and so on. You should be able to watch a machinima movie and enjoy it for all the things it's meant to convey, not the technical details of how it was made. All those details should be transparent. We are just beginning to see machinima films that leave these game roots behind.'

KEN THAIN, *Machinimator*

PUSHING THE BOUNDARIES: EXPERIMENTAL MACHINIMA

There are some pieces of machinima that defy conventional description. Fountainhead's award-winning *Anna* is a *Fantasia*-style short story about the cycle of life, told from the point of view of a flower. *Anthem*, by French artist Julien Vanhoenacker, now Senior Animator at Digital Magic in Bangkok, is a disturbing piece about pain and suffering. *Scrap*, created by Folklore Studios for the Make Something Unreal Contest, is almost balletic, reminiscent of Tim Burton's *The Nightmare Before Christmas*. *Halla*, by Finnish company Moppi Productions, is a lyrically shot fairytale, almost like a digital Jan Svankmajer film. Maine-based Richard de Costa's innovative sci-fi epic, *K'ai, Death of Dreams*, married the disparate worlds of opera and machinima to create what he calls 'the first true space opera'.

However, perhaps the most impressive use of machinima is when machinimators create something that looks nothing like a game, or indeed nothing like a 3D world at all. Visually, they are no different to any other form of animation, giving little or no clue to their gaming heritage.

Probably the finest exponent of this form of machinima is the German machinimator and conventional film-maker Friedrich Kirschner. His award-winning films, *The Tournament* and *The Journey*, are strange, haunting, pieces that are almost abstract in their look. The characters seem as if they are drawn by hand, floating on a painted backdrop, and there is no hint of 3D, photorealism, or gamey action.

Another award-winning example of radical machinima is the music video *Fake Science* by Dead on Que. The sets look two-dimensional, and the detail is minimal throughout, creating a stark, modernist style like Eastern European animation of the 1970s.

IX, another stunning film from Moppi, is a surreal music video, a strange, trippy tram journey in a world of magazine cut-outs. 'No reason. No story. Just watch', says creator Mikko Mononen.

Films like *IX* and *The Journey* aren't to everyone's taste, but neither are the films of Godfrey Reggio or Kihachiro Kawamoto. But they are nevertheless challenging pieces: challenging the viewer to think about the issues they raise, and technically challenging the boundaries of their art.

'Machinima is like a kid with a video camera. It's exploration.'

JAKE HUGHES, *Machinimator*

© Moppi Productions   © Moppi Productions

The award-winning **Fake Science** (2002, RIGHT), by Dead on Que, and the surreal **IX** (2004, LEFT), by Moppi Productions, take divergence from game imagery and game culture to the extreme.

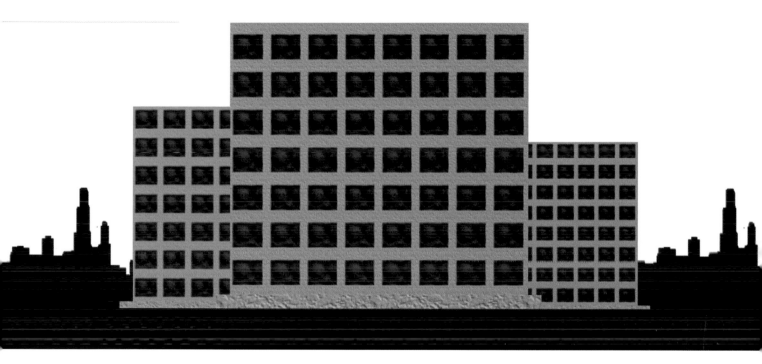

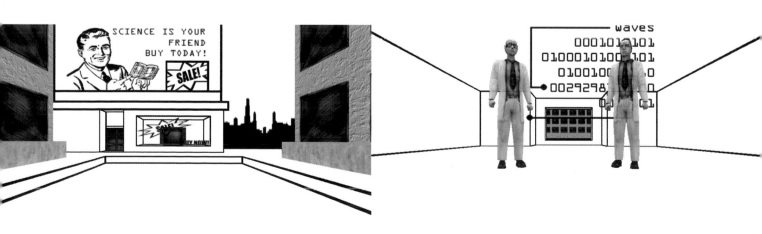

CASE STUDY:
THE JOURNEY

**Friedrich 'Fiezi' Kirschner produces some of the most breathtaking and unique pieces of machinima.
He gives us an insight into the way he works.**

I did short films and a lot of editing prior to machinima.
I decided to go into the virtual world mainly because of
resources. Film-making needs a lot of people and a lot of money.

The idea to do machinima struck me when watching the
cut-scenes of the *Aliens vs Predator 2* game from Monolith.
I realized that it would be a great way to tell stories, like
in comics or animated series. It seemed easier to me than
'traditional' 3D animation. I get pretty scared of 3DS Max and
Maya with those tons of windows, options, and preferences.
I like the modular approach of splitting up everything you do
into little tasks and then bringing them all together, reusing a
lot of things you do. Machinima seemed a lot more non-linear
to me than 3D animation does. To me it's more like editing. I
don't make up a big plan when editing a short film. You arrange
your shots according to the script, then refine and rearrange
until you're happy with it. Machinima is a lot like that.

I think in pictures and I need to see them on screen, so
I can work with them and refine them. Realtime is absolutely
necessary for the way I work. I couldn't wait 20 minutes to see
what my five-second animation looks like. I want to hit play and
watch it. Call me impatient if you like!

Another benefit of machinima is the look itself. Although
I don't like most computer games' looks, they still seem warmer
than most 3D animation that I come across. Most 3D animated
scenes look too clean to me.

My latest film, *The Journey*, was based on a goodnight story
I made up a couple of years ago. As a written story, it never really
worked. (Well, people fell asleep – does that count?) It relied too
much on visual description of what's going on. When my little
cousin was born, I decided to convert it into a film he could
watch – while he's still a child, when he grows up, and finally
when he's a teen – and still find different things he might like.

The whole film, from idea to full completion, took about
two months. On my first films I used a lot of in-game assets,
replacing only a few textures, animations, and decorative
meshes. On *The Journey*, everything was created from scratch.
I won't use any more in-game assets in the future.

The soundtrack was improvised after the film was half-
done. It was a one-night session with a friend playing cello and
another one recording her in his apartment. I cannot stress
enough how vital the soundtrack is for machinima as well as
films in general. It makes up 50% of the show.

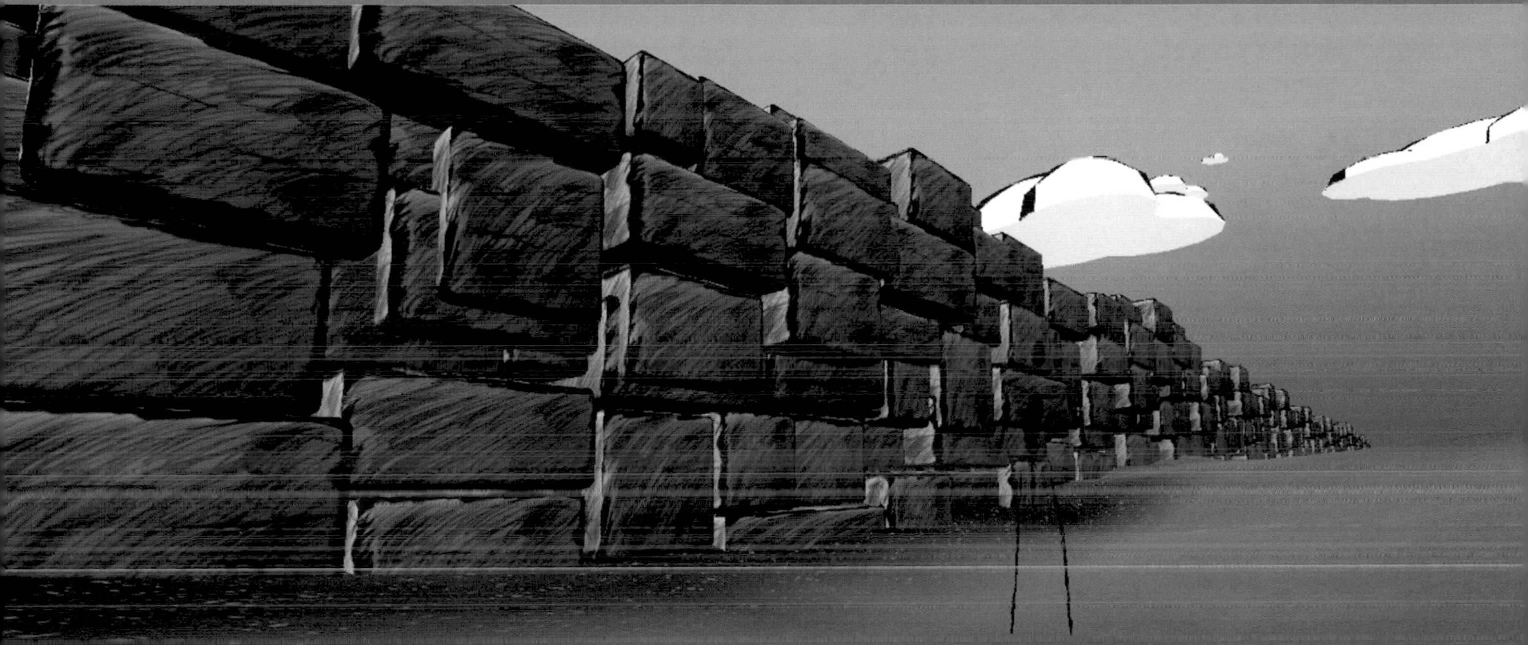

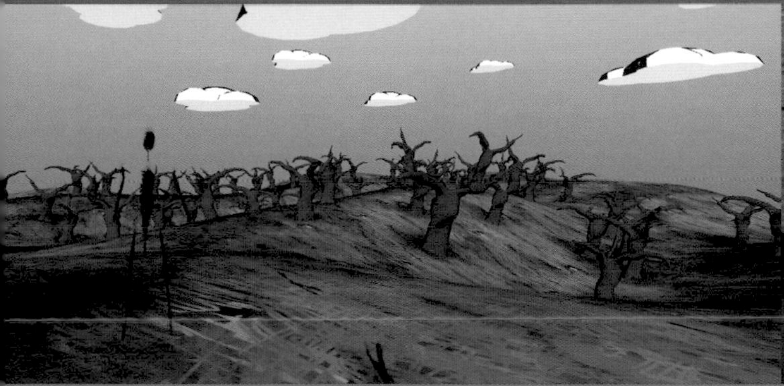

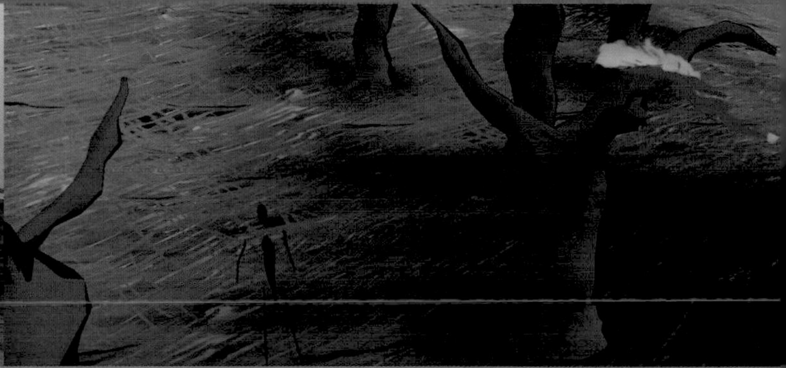

MACHINIMA COMES OF AGE

'**Machinima does compete with traditional animation. The very fact that it is held up against traditional animated films for judgement of "acceptable animation" is a competitive judgement.**'

KEN THAIN, *Machinimator*

Machinima is beginning to move away from being just a hobby artform to a commercial proposition. In October 2004, Rooster Teeth, the team behind the *Halo* fan series *Red vs Blue*, announced that they were being sponsored by game industry giants Electronic Arts to produce *The Strangerhood*, a series of short online machinima films set in the suburban world of *The Sims 2*. EA was aware of the extent to which *Red vs Blue* had bolstered the *Halo* community and was keen to see Rooster Teeth do the same for *The Sims*. Not only is *The Strangerhood* an

entertaining piece of reality TV set in EA's virtual world, but it acts as a high-profile showcase for the film-making tools built into the game.

Strange Company, the leader in commercial machinima, uses the technique to produce corporate videos and to create short films for the BBC. 'In the last few years, we've done a parody piece for the BBC, a presentation piece for a pharmaceutical company, and a show for BAFTA [British Academy of Film and Television Arts], among others,'

'There's a growing trend for people to buy the television series and movies they love direct on DVD. Machinima is a great opportunity to sidestep the conventional film industry. There's the potential to build up an excellent direct-to-audience culture.'

PETER RASMUSSEN, *Machinimator*

LEFT: **Game On** *(2004), sponsored by Volvo, marks a major collaboration between machinima and the world of mainstream advertising.*
BELOW: **The Strangerhood** *(2004), produced by* **Red vs Blue** *veterans Rooster Teeth, was endorsed by videogame publishers Electronic Arts to promote* **The Sims 2**.
BELOW FAR LEFT: **Matrix 4x1** *(2000), created by Strange Company, was one of the first commercial machinima.*

comments Hugh Hancock. 'We're not really advertising our services, so we're getting interest by a word-of-mouth process, which brings us some really interesting clients. In general, wherever someone wants to make a film that looks like a game, or wants to produce an animated character piece cheaply, we're in with a chance.'

Partly fuelled by the desire to make money from their work, and partly by the need to break free of the limitations of online distribution, the first commercial machinima DVDs are beginning to make an appearance. There are three seasons of *Red vs Blue* available via their website, and in 2004, Peter Rasmussen released his highly successful *Killer Robot* via www.machinima.com. Jake Hughes' feature-length film *Anachronox*, based on the game by Ion Storm and created from the cut-scenes in the game, has been eagerly awaited by

machinima fans and game fans alike. The great advantage of DVD is that the viewer can see the film at full quality, including surround sound, subtitles, and all the other features audiences have come to expect in a modern product. For longer features, such as those mentioned above, the viewer can watch all the way through without having to download the parts one at a time and reassemble them on their computer.

The most interesting development is the way in which machinima is slowly but surely becoming integrated into mainstream media. Although these are early days, there are signs that machinima will become accepted alongside other forms of animation and film-making as a useful creative tool. By playing to the strengths of machinima, and using other techniques to counteract its limitations, film-makers stand to benefit both creatively and financially.

MACHINIMA ON TV

The relationship between games and TV has always been uneasy. Television companies are acutely aware that when people are playing games, they're not watching television, and their advertising revenue suffers as a result. Animation companies producing TV-quality animation often deride game animation for its comparatively low quality. On the other hand, gaming is a huge part of popular culture, and TV companies ignore it at their peril.

Few companies have been as innovative in their marriage between television and games as the BBC. It has broadcast a range of shows that use gaming technology to create programs that straddle the line between linear and non-linear entertainment.

Fightbox, which aired in 2003–2004, was a televised games contest. In the early rounds, players fought online gladiatorial battles between creatures that they created from a freely downloadable kit supplied by the BBC. The most successful players were then selected for the televised finals. The players went head to head on their computers via a Local Area Network (LAN), but instead of showing the contest as it appeared on-screen to the players, the characters were digitally extracted from the game and matted into the studio set so that, to the viewer at home, they appeared to be fighting in a huge arena in front of a live audience.

Bamzooki used a similar idea, but was aimed at much younger viewers. Contestants created their own 'Zooks' from a downloadable kit designed by Gameware Development and based on animals found in the real world. However, unlike the creatures in *Fightbox*, the Zooks were designed to be semi-autonomous and were an experiment in simple artificial life. They then competed in a variety of tests, designed to demonstrate strength, agility, and endurance. Again, the Zooks were digitally mapped onto the studio set so they appeared to be competing in front of their young creators.

The most famous example of game technology on television is *Time Commanders*. This show takes members of the public and places them in the roles of the commanders of famous ancient battles, such as the Roman Paulinus facing Boudicca's revolt, or Ramses II at the battle of Qadesh. The battle is displayed on a giant screen and takes place in realtime while the players issue commands verbally to their troops via

'The more we head to the future, the more we'll be thinking about integrating realtime and pre-rendered assets. Of course, in the world of linear entertainment, no one cares how you've made your imagery – it had just better be great!'

LORNE LANNING, *President, Oddworld Inhabitants*

Bamzooki (LEFT) and *Fightbox* (ABOVE) show the innovative ways in which game technology is being used to create television programmes.

expert computer operators. The battles are created entirely using the Creative Assembly game *Rome: Total War*. The game provides not only the visual imagery, ranging from eagle's eye views of the battlefield to close-up shots of troops in combat or lying in ambush, but also provides the opposition, using authentic battle tactics of the era to control the enemy troops. The show has been a smash hit among gamers and history buffs alike, and when the game was released in September 2004, it was a huge success.

'The show was originally the conception of Adam McDonald, our development executive, who wanted to come up with a way of allowing people to fight ancient battles from history. The difficulty was how to achieve it. After some consideration I felt that our usual paths of live action or full CG wouldn't work for either timescale or budget reasons. I then came up with the idea of trying to co-opt a game engine', says producer Cassian Harrison, from Lion Television.

Ian Ruxborough of Creative Assembly explains how it works. 'Most of what you see in the final cut was actually what happened in the studio. *Total War* games feature the ability to save the battles and then replay them. For *Rome*, we expanded this to enable camera tracks to be laid in over the replays. This meant that the editors could watch the studio battles over and over again and then pick and choose the moments

they wanted to show, and where they wanted the camera to be. Then it was just a matter of rendering out the footage into a stream of TGA files ready for use in the edit suite. We didn't have to change anything significant – it was more just little bits and bobs to make the show work. For example, we introduced spectator modes so that machines that were not directly controlling an army could still view the action and display it on the big screen in the studio.

'I am extremely pleased that we were able to get gaming technology and visuals onto TV in a prime slot without making a show that feels geeky and for computer nerds only. Although our core audience is probably male skewed, I think we managed to make the source of the visuals subsidiary to the human narrative and competition of the shows – basically it is about people, not technology,' concludes Harrison.

A similar use of game technology, although in a very different way, was to create battle scenes for the series *Battlefield Britain*. The programme integrated live footage of small groups of re-enactors with machinima-generated footage of full-scale armies to show how the battles flowed while retaining the close-up feel of what it was like to be in the midst of the action. 'I didn't think of it as gaming technology. I thought of it as what you'd see in Hollywood but done for television', commented series producer Danielle Peck.

LEFT: **Time Commanders**
ABOVE: **Battlefield Britain**

MACHINIMA IN HOLLYWOOD

'You could actually see in realtime how everything would look. And you could record the animation as you moved the camera around, so it was like being on a set. When I went back to 3D animation, I missed that.'

RANDY COLE, *Animator*

Machinima is even making itself felt in the megabudget world of the films. Leading film-makers such as Steven Spielberg, George Lucas, and James Cameron take advantage of the speed and cheapness of machinima to change the way they work.

On the 2001 film *A.I.*, lead concept designer Wilson Tang created *Rouge City* as a complete virtual world, known as a 3D animatic. Spielberg used this to decide exactly which camera angles would be required for each shot. This in turn told the set builders and model-makers exactly what they needed

to create, and what would be off-camera. In one example, the characters enter a vehicle and fly up out of the city. Spielberg chose to place the camera low down, pointing up at the vehicle, so no street level detail was required. 'If Steven had said, "I want the camera pointing down", it would have affected everything,' pointed out Tang.

But the *A.I.* team went further than just 3D animatics by grafting on a customized game engine that allowed them to mimic cameras, complete with focal lengths, aspect ratios, camera heights, cranes, and helicopter shots. Spielberg used this game world to familiarize himself with the locations. Seth Rosenthal, set visualization supervisor at Industrial Light & Magic, created a system allowing the team to blend live action actors, miniatures, and computer-generated imagery from the 3D world, and see in realtime what they would look like. After the live action and miniatures shots had been filmed, the CG animation team replaced all the realtime animation elements with high-quality animation rendered offline using conventional tools and techniques.

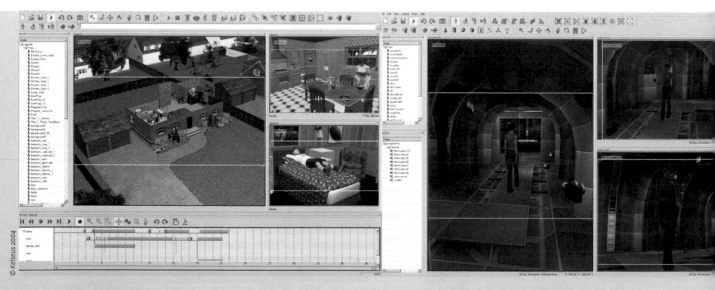

© Kelseus 2004

ABOVE: **Antics** *is the first commercial-grade machinima tool targeted at the Hollywood previsualization market.*

'It lets the director come up with a better idea than what he previsualized, and everybody on set sees it. We created shots that were different from the storyboards. That's a big creative plus.'

DENNIS MUREN, *Visual Effects Designer, ILM*

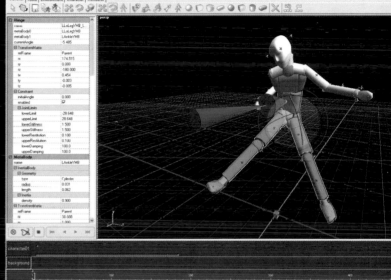

ILM now uses machinima as a standard tool for previsualization. On the recent *Star Wars* films, they created a customized version of *Unreal Tournament* to assist George Lucas in creating an animated storyboard.

In the UK, Cambridge-based company Kelseus decided to focus its machinima tool *Antics Pre-Viz* exclusively on the previsualization market. 'This will transform animation production processes,' opines Professor John Vince, Head of Computer Animation Academic Group at Bournemouth University. Instead of creating storyboards that consist of stills like a comic book, Antics allows the film-makers to make their entire film in rough, quickly and easily. Using tools that are as intuitive as a videogame, the director can control the action, place and move cameras, rehearse timings, and even do a rough edit of the film, without needing to be an animator, and without needing to construct sets or call in actors. This translates into a huge cost saving, as the production team only need to shoot the shots and construct the areas of the set that they know they will need. The chance of having to cut complete scenes from the film is dramatically reduced, since the director and producer can see the whole film before they start filming.

The saving for even simple sequences is significant, but for complex shots, the potential for machinima is only just beginning to be exploited. Setting up a major stunt sequence such as a car chase is one of the most time-consuming things for a film crew to do. The excitement of this sort of scene comes from the breathless action, the dramatic camera angles, and the movement. These are all aspects that are very hard to convey through stills. More importantly, filming a stunt sequence, particularly if it involves closing off a major city street, is usually a one-shot affair – if it doesn't go right on the day, there may well be no opportunity to do it again. Using machinima allows stunt supervisors to work with directors to determine exactly what an action sequence will look like and how to get it before a single camera rolls.

The crossover between game and film extends to the tools used to create the onscreen visuals. In Peter Jackson's *Lord of the Rings*, the huge armies of elves and orcs were created using *Massive*. Instead of having to animate each character individually, the soldiers were virtual actors who existed in a game-type environment and performed according to a script. In the recent swords and sandals blockbuster *Troy*, many of the action sequences were created by The Moving Picture Company using virtual stuntmen in NaturalMotion's *Endorphin*. This is the very same tool that was recently used by Namco to create the videogame *Tekken 5*.

MACHINIMA AND MUSIC

The music industry is always eager to engage with popular culture and adopt the idioms and fashions of other media. As videogames become a common language of people of music-buying age rather than just a pastime enjoyed by a few nerds, the marriage of commercial music and game imagery seems to be somehow inevitable.

The first official bond of music and machinima arrived with Ken Thain's *Rebel vs Thug*, produced in 2002 for New York rappers Fine Arts Militia featuring Chuck D. 'The band was looking for someone who could create a cutting-edge music video,' remembers Thain. 'They were very upfront that this was an unsigned band and not a paying gig, but an opportunity for a machinima film-maker to get some exposure in the medium. I liked the sound of it and was fine that there was no budget involved. After all, this was an inherent strength with machinima, "zero budget production". They had a song that would go well with the raw, unpolished visual edge of a machinima film.

'Early on in the project I decided to go with traditional 3D animation as the creative influence the band was having on the video was surpassing the possibilities of what could be done in machinima. But after about six months of work in traditional 3D with minimal progress, and with some advances within the capabilities of machinima, I decided to revert to machinima development. I had to take advantage of the production benefits of machinima to get the video done and because the scope of the video would simply not be possible in traditional 3D without a professional budget. This worked well in the end, as the machinima influence provided a strong visual style that accompanied the song. Now in watching the video, especially at the time of release, it provides the audience with a very questionable line over what is visually the result of it being a machinima video and what was intended to give it a raw, machinima feel.'

Video director Tommy Pallotta followed with the award-winning video *In the Waiting Line*, created for British band Zero 7. Made in collaboration with Fountainhead, and using their *Machinimation* tool, the teams worked together to combine their expertise in music video, programming, and game engines. 'I was invited to speak at the L.A. Film Festival and on that trip I met Tommy Pallotta,' says Fountainhead's Katherine Anna Kang. 'We got into a conversation about machinima and he was the first and only film-maker there who actually understood what I was talking about. Rather than a blank expression of the dazed and confused with polite uh-huh's, he really got it.' MTV described the video as 'an enigmatically experimental visual experience that tells the story of a lonely robot's search for meaning and emancipation from the routine of daily existence in outer space'. Fountainhead also took advantage of the 3D world created for the video to produce a game using the same models.

MTV has continued to blur the boundaries of games, music, and television with the recent series *Video Mods*. Created by Big Bear Entertainment, the show recreates music videos from artists including Christina Milian, Von Bondies, Evanescence, and Black Eyed Peas, but using game characters from games such as *The Sims, Bloodrayne 2*, and *Tribes* in place of the original human actors. The series has proved popular with viewers and games publishers alike. 'We've gotten plenty of publishers eager to sign up their characters for new episodes', says creator Tony Schiff. While the first series was all pre-rendered video, plans are in place with sponsors NVIDIA to start shifting to realtime technology for special live events, based on machinima software that Schiff is developing.

Machinima music videos: *In the Waiting Line* (2003, ABOVE), by Fountainhead Entertainment, made with **Quake 3** and **Machinimation**. *Rebel vs Thug* (2002, BELOW), by Ken Thain, filmed in **Quake 2** using **Keygrip2**.

MACHINIMA AWARDS AND FESTIVALS

Award-winning machinima: **UT XMP** (2004, *LEFT*), by Free Monkeys (**Unreal Tournament 2004**) and **Bouncer Please** (2004, *ABOVE*), by Binary Pictures (**Quake 2**).

RIGHT: The Machinima Film Festival 2003. The ILL Clan perform live machinima to a packed house. Uwe Girlich sees how **Anna** was produced.

'It's a gift to be able to see new media being created; it's like watching Gutenberg as he invented the printing press.'

HENRY LOWOOD, *Curator for the history of science and technology, Stanford University Libraries*

'We will listen to the machinima community in the same way as we listen to the modders. We simply have too much fun watching your work not to!'

JOHAN PERSSON, *Creative Director, Digital Illusions*

As machinima grows in popularity, among viewers and creators, it's natural that there should be awards and contests to honour the best. In September 2004, the prestigious Ottawa International Animation Festival included a machinima category for the first time, screening machinima films alongside traditional 2D and 3D animation, and other new media, such as Flash films made for the Web.

The more avant-garde multimedia Resfest is a global travelling film festival, which in 2004 visited 33 cities in 13 countries from Australia to South Africa, Brazil, and Scotland. Hamburg's Bitfilm festival includes a machinima category alongside other new media animation. The Sundance Online Film Festival has opened its doors to machinima films. And at the 2004 Florida Film Festival, the ILL Clan performed machinima live in front of the audience, using their characters Larry and Lenny Lumberjack as co-hosts of the award ceremony.

By far the most important festival for machinimators, though, is the annual Machinima Film Festival, run by the Academy of Machinima Arts & Sciences in New York, and sponsored by graphics card makers NVIDIA. With categories including Best Picture, Best Direction, Best Virtual Performance, Best Visual Design, Best Sound, Best Writing, Best Editing, Best Technical Achievement, Best Commercial/ Game Machinima, and Best Independent Film, it truly celebrates the machinimator's art.

NVIDIA also co-sponsors the other major contest for machinimators, Epic's Make Something Unreal Contest. This popular contest includes categories for all sorts of mods to *Unreal Tournament 2004*. The machinima category provides a welcome opportunity for machinimators to show how far they can push the envelope with the *Matinee* tool. 'The quality of the machinima Make Something Unreal Contest entries continues to increase', says contest organizer Jeff Morris. 'Recent entries have included some very involved and effective stories. We are really impressed by the entries that really push the technology, that accomplish things that Epic never envisioned. It's a new form of animation and linear storytelling. Once people find the kinds of stories that work best in realtime, the sky's the limit.'

Epic is not alone among game developers in providing this level of support to machinima: *City of Heroes*, NCSoft's MMORPG based in the superhero genre; *Second Life*, a freeform MMORPG created by Linden Research; and film noir shooter *Max Payne 2* from Rockstar are all searching for the next John Woo or Martin Scorsese.

The lure of fame, glory, and riches has undoubtedly spurred machinimators on to greater heights. But there's more on offer than just 15 minutes of fame and a free PC. 'This is a great recruiting resource for our own company and those who license Epic technology', points out Morris.

THE FUTURE OF MACHINIMA

'What's it going to take to create the first machinima breakthrough? A decent budget.'

KATHERINE ANNA KANG, *Fountainhead Entertainment*

Right now, machinima is a new, and slightly strange way to create films. It's so up-and-coming that most people haven't even heard of the word, let alone know what it means, and even fewer have seen a machinima film. A machinimator is someone rare.

But a decade from now, machinima will almost certainly be just one of the many techniques in the film-maker's arsenal. Just as the CGI experts were assimilated into the industry ten years ago, so the machinima experts will go in their turn. The machinima-generated special effects that were ground-breaking and expensive on *Troy* and *Lord of the Rings* will become commonplace for television. Machinimators will take their place alongside the 3D modellers, the compositors, and the texture artists in the digital effects houses of the future. Controlling a virtual character within a 3D game world will be as valuable a skill as being a supporting actor.

And just as hand-drawn 2D animation gave way to computer-generated 2D animation, and now even that is giving way to 3D animation, so traditional 3D animation will inevitably give way, in part, to machinima. 'I don't know if Hollywood will call it machinima when they do it, but it will be machinima nonetheless', says Anthony Bailey, of the Academy of Machinima Arts & Sciences.

That may seem like an ambitious vision. Machinima still has a long way to go. Not even the best game engine available in 2004 can compete with the visual quality of *Shrek 2*. But just look at what's on the way. The new generation of video cards will produce levels of realism undreamed of even a few years ago – and they'll be doing it all in realtime on your home computer. Game engines will be using physics models that a few years ago existed only in top-end simulators. We'll have automatic lip synch that will make characters look like they're really speaking, and we'll have models that can display complex emotions. The constraints on machinima will cease to be the technological limits. Instead, they'll be down to the time, the money, and the skill put into the projects.

There's never been a more exciting time to become a machinimator!

'While many of the machinima people talk about it as a new way to make films, I think there's something very prescient about it. It's telling us what films in the future might be like. The camera is reduced to a construct, to one's perspective onscreen rather than a physical object. It's truer to the notion of digital cinema than using digital cameras.'

CARL GOODMAN, *Curator for digital media, American Museum of the Moving Image*

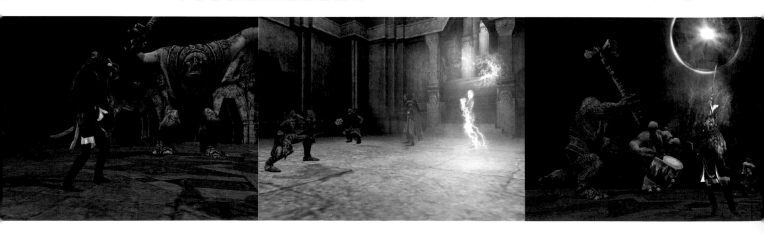

When games look this good, the
future for machinima is bright.
LEFT: **Lord of the Rings, the Third
Age** (2004), from Electronic Arts.
ABOVE: **Half-Life 2** (2004), by Valve.

MAKING MACHINIMA

Machinima is an artform as diverse as animation or film-making, not just in the creative sense, but also in the technical sense. Just as there are many ways to create animation, ranging from zoetropes and simple hand-drawn pencil sketches to cels, rotoscoping, stop-motion, and full CGI, so there are many different ways to create machinima. Each requires its own skills and tools, and each produces different results.

Although the various techniques all have their fans and their detractors, it is important to recognize that none offers the perfect solution. The simple charms of *Gertie the Dinosaur* are very different to the documentary accuracy of the highly detailed creatures in *Walking With Dinosaurs*, the saccharine cuteness of Alodar in Disney's *Dinosaur*, the visceral aggression of the tyrannosaurs in *Fantasia*, or the dated but still entertaining stop-motion jerkiness of Harryhausen's *Valley of Gwangi*. The choice of technique is stylistic, not scientific.

'If you think of machinima as Puppetry 2.0, the advantages become a lot clearer. Because these are CG characters, we can give them a lot more visual appeal than conventional puppets, and we can hand bits of their control over to the computer. Also, we can take advantage of the things that CG does really well – epic vistas, impossible situations, unlimited set and costume budget.'

HUGH HANCOCK, *Strange Company*

'Machinima has been compared to puppet shows, animated films, improvisational theatre, and interactive fiction. In fact, machinima is all those things.'

BARBARA ROBERTSON, *Computer Graphics World*

*A completely functional film studio inside a videogame: **The Movies** (2005), by Lionhead.*

PART 2

WHY MAKE MACHINIMA?

BECAUSE YOU CAN

The greatest attraction of machinima is that starting is so easy. It is not necessary to invest in expensive tools or equipment to create high-quality film; given a reasonably up-to-date computer, you can set up the rest of your virtual film studio for next to nothing. Although there are professional-quality tools for just about every part of the process, there are freeware or budget alternatives to all of them. Compared with the cost of buying cameras, lights, microphones, and all the other equipment required to make 'real' films, it's perfect for a beginner to learn the craft of film-making without breaking the bank.

Technically, machinima is an almost completely level playing field. It's not like the difference between using the professional gear that George Lucas uses on *Star Wars* and using a DV camera bought from a big box store. Everyone has equal access to practically the same tools. While using professional tools such as *3D Studio Max* or *Maya*, rather than the budget tool *Milkshape*, does have advantages, it's not the key factor to obtaining quality. The visual quality that a novice can produce from the *Doom 3* engine is identical to the visual quality that the most experienced machinimator can produce. Crystal clear footage at 25 frames per second running in 1024 x 768 resolution is for everyone. The skill is in using the tools to get the best out of them, and having the vision in the first place to create a film that people want to watch.

And unlike making real films, the machinimator can work completely solo. Armed with a copy of *The Sims 2* or *Unreal Tournament 2004*, the machinimator can create the entire piece from beginning to end without needing to drag in actors, crew, animators, or anyone else. This is another great attraction for amateurs. Novice directors can make as many mistakes as they like, or change their minds more often than they change their socks, without hearing the groans of cast and crew as they call for the fourteenth reshoot of the same scene. Film-making can be fitted in around work, school, or family commitments, snatching the odd 15 minutes here and there to film a short sequence or tweak the editing.

'It really takes some time to create something amazing, maybe longer than you expected. The good thing about machinima is, you can get started pretty fast. The bad thing is, if you want to make something decent, it takes you quite a while.'
FRIEDRICH 'FIEZI' KIRSCHNER, *Machinimator*

Machinima is also enormously flexible. The rest of this section will show that there are many different ways to create machinima. As the medium develops, and machinimators are developing new tools and new techniques, it provides a wonderful environment for experimentation and innovation. Just as animators found they could do things that live action film-makers couldn't, and animators working with computers realized they could make films that hand animators couldn't, so machinimators are beginning to explore new territories.

Perhaps the greatest advantage of working in machinima is that the game engine provides the novice with enough to start making films right away. It's not necessary to know the first thing about 3D modelling, texturing, animation, or even lighting. By using the assets already supplied in the original game, the machinimator can bypass many of the most technically demanding tasks and start capturing footage immediately. 'Look at the pieces done in *Far Cry* by Paul Soldera', comments machinimator Nathan Moller. 'He's just working on his own, alone, without any custom animations or meshes, but squeezes very entertaining little tidbits of video from it. He's not trying to be the next *Red vs Blue* or ILL Clan, he just does what he can do with what he's got.'

‘I've always been an aspiring film-maker and a lifelong game player ... you spend enough time doing anything, eventually it just comes together.’

BURNIE BURNS, *Machinimator, creator of* **Red vs Blue**

ABOVE: **Valerie** (2004), by Paul Soldera, created in Crytek's **Far Cry**.
BELOW: **The Return** (2004), filmed by Ted Brown using Ritual Entertainment's **Heavy Metal FAKK 2**, is an unusual but highly effective choice of game engine.

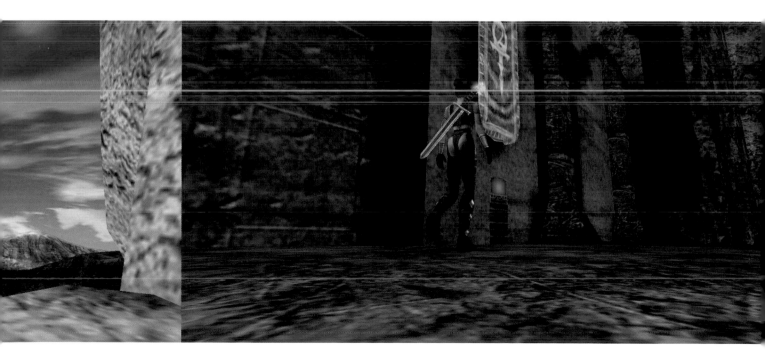

CASE STUDY: *STRANGE COMPANY*

Edinburgh-based Strange Company is the UK's foremost machinima crew. Founded in 1997 by Hugh Hancock, it has made the machinima community what it is today. We caught up with Hancock in the middle of preproduction on his latest venture, *Bloodspell*, being filmed in *Neverwinter Nights*.

Machinima and traditional animation are totally different artforms. Machinima isn't animation. Machinima is the spiritual successor to Supermarionation – indeed, the main difference between the two is that machinima takes place inside a computer. Machinima is a fantastic choice for an independent film-maker who wants to make epic films without having to acquire $120 million first.

I don't think that whether machinima can compete with animation or not should be the issue. We've gotten way too focused on CG animation because it's superficially closest to the machinima artform.

To give an example – can Digital Video compete with CG? Well, there's no arguing that *Blair Witch* or *Dogville* isn't as pretty as *Finding Nemo*, but I don't think that's going to stop Miramax picking up the latest DV brilliance. It's the same thing with machinima – what matters is whether the audience will watch it.

And machinima offers something that that audience has rarely seen. High-budget films and series – science-fiction, action, fantasy – are well-known to suffer from a lack of risk-taking, a lack of the kind of bold spirit that makes their literary equivalents so gripping. That's for a very good reason – if you gave me $120 million to make a film, and told me I had to make it back, I'd be cautious too. And thus we get focus groups, and blockbuster movies, and all the experimental, interesting, risk-taking film-making condemned to the low-budget ghetto – where it's damn near impossible to compete with *Star Wars*, say.

Using machinima, I can create a film on the scale of *Star Wars* in under two years, part-time, no budget. And it would be easily high-enough quality to capture audiences' attention.

Strange Company is making a feature-length fantasy film right now, called *Bloodspell*. On a three-figure budget. And I guarantee that while it'll be rough round the edges, and not as polished as a Hollywood production – just like any other indie film – it's got ideas in there that you'd never see in a Hollywood film, because you could never get sign-off from the focus groups, the executives, and the entire massive decision-making apparatus.

That's why I've been making machinima for seven years now, and why I believe machinima has the potential to revolutionize the medium of film – by pushing it much closer to Francis Ford Coppola's vision of film as a democratic medium.

As for the aesthetic – yeah, currently games players 'get' machinima more easily, because they're used to the game aesthetic. That's changing by the minute, though, as gaming becomes more widespread.

TOP LEFT: ***Ozymandias*** *(2002)*
TOP RIGHT: ***Steelwight*** *(2002)*
CENTRE: ***Bloodspell*** *(2005)*
BOTTOM: ***Arcoxia*** *(2002)*

LIMITATIONS OF MACHINIMA

There are some things that machinima can't do, and areas where it doesn't make the grade when compared to animation or live-action film-making. Despite the protestations and grand aspirations of some machinimators, it's unlikely that we'll see a machinima production achieving the dizzy heights of a *Finding Nemo* or a *Lord of the Rings* any time soon. 'In its production mechanics and the cost-per-minute graph, machinima is TV, not film,' points out veteran machinimator Anthony Bailey.

The greatest drawback is that while machinima is excellent for generating high-octane action sequences that would be prohibitively expensive for either conventional animation or live action, it is less effective when it comes to characters simply walking and talking. Blowing up an oil tanker is easy; a character blowing his nose or opening a bottle of wine is comparatively hard. Few games supply the machinimator with a sufficient range of facial gestures and body positions to achieve the range of emotions that a hand-animated character or actor can perform. A subtle half-smile, a belly laugh, or even sitting at a table with one hand resting on the chin are beyond the scope of most game engines.

'Machinima's strengths – fast production time and scale – are pretty much wiped out by trying to achieve hand-quality animation,' agrees Hugh Hancock. 'Trying to match conventional animation in those terms is unfortunately a fast train to matching the production times of conventional animation too, and that's not playing to machinima's strength – the ability to tell complex, expansive stories on a realistic timeframe and budget.'

It's not that the game engines can't achieve this level of animation. It's just that game developers see no reason to provide it. Game players are generally interested in their ability to run, jump, and shoot, not to be a virtual Johnny Depp while they do it. With game budgets spiralling ever higher, game companies focus their development efforts on gameplay, not on possible side benefits to machinimators.

Change is slowly, but surely, taking place. Games companies frequently create facial expressions and body language for the cut-scenes in their games, and making these available with the game code is easy enough. *Half-Life 2*, from Valve Software, includes *Face Power*, a tool reportedly designed specifically for machinima. The characters have a range of facial expressions built in, and forty muscles that machinimators can control directly to create custom expressions. 'Animation is desperately expensive right now, but there's every reason to think that one or both of physics-model based generation or affordable motion capture can bring the price right down,' says Bailey.

Other machinimators address the limitations by creating custom tools. Strange Company uses a tool called *TOGLFaceS* (Take Over GL Face Skins) to give characters in *Neverwinter Nights* a range of emotions that weren't in the original game.

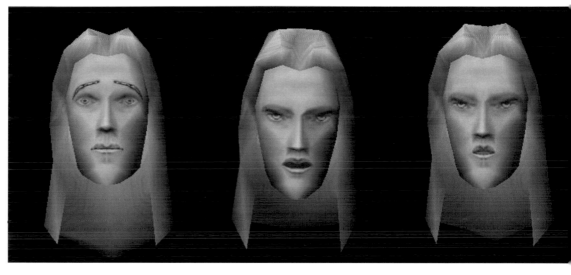

BELOW: **Who's On First** (2004), by OC3 Entertainment, uses **Unreal Tournament 2004** to recreate a classic black and white Abbott and Costello sketch. It uses the company's **Impersonator** tool to generate high-quality lip synch.

ABOVE: Different facial expressions for the same character in **Bloodspell** (2005), using Strange Company's **TOGLFaceS** utility: fear, anger, and distrust.

'As game engine technology progresses, the lack of expression is something that will be less of a problem, but I think it is something that can be handled with a few novel ideas.'

ATUSSA SIMON, Machinimator

Atussa Simon uses similar techniques in *The Battle of Xerxes*. Essentially, the characters have a library of faces with different expressions, and the machinimators can switch between them at will, either in realtime or by pausing the action and changing the face, like giving an actor a range of masks to convey different emotions. It is a simple theatrical technique, but is often sufficient for conveying enough emotion to tell the story. Most Japanese anime made for television relies on a very small range of stock facial expressions and minimal detail to convey emotion, yet this has not stopped *Pokemon*, *Dragon Ball Z*, and the like becoming hugely successful across the world.

'90% of movement in live film is head motion. That's even true in conventional animation,' Hancock points out. 'Hanna-Barbera's limited animation style is often decried by animators – I've heard it described as "the worst animation ever produced on TV" – but if you asked 50 people to name their favorite cartoons, *The Flintstones*, *Scooby Doo*, *Top Cat*, and so on would be high on the list. The best machinima works because of intelligent camera work, well-used, minimal spot animation, and a strong story. And all the evidence suggests that, above all, a strong story is what audiences want to watch.'

MACHINIMA TECHNIQUES

Machinima is not a homogeneous art. In its way, it is as diverse as animation in its widest sense. In terms of tools, techniques, and skills, there is little in common between the plasticine stop-motion modelling of *Wallace and Gromit*, and the high-tech computer wizardry of *Ice Age*. Similarly, machinima such as *Bot* and *The River* require completely different approaches.

There are four main techniques to creating machinima. Each has its advantages and disadvantages. They require different tools, different skills, and different engines. A studio set up to create one type of machinima will look nothing like a studio for creating another.

The simplest form of machinima is more akin to reality television than drama. The machinimator does not create the story or script in advance, but allows the game's inbuilt AI (artifical intelligence) to control and direct the characters. The machinimator then acts as a documentary cameraman or reporter to record the events as they unfold.

In order to take control of the story, and work to a script, the machinimator needs to be able to direct the action and the actors with some degree of precision. The simplest

solution is for each character in a scene to be controlled by a real person, like a virtual puppet, and follow the director's instructions, exactly like a live film set. One or more people act as cameramen, and the director records the action as it appears on their screens.

A new level of flexibility is added to this puppeteering approach by taking advantage of the demo format of some games to use a technique called 'recamming'. Although the characters are still human-controlled initially, the director can subsequently manipulate the recording in many different ways. New characters can be added, or characters deleted. Cameras can be moved and refocused, or lights repositioned. One character can even be recostumed or substituted for another without needing to reshoot the scene.

The most powerful approach is in some respects the fully scripted technique. In this, the puppeteering element is dropped entirely, and the entire film is created programmatically, in the form of story data. Every movement and every gesture is defined by issuing a series of instructions to the characters, which they then carry out with frame-perfect and pixel-perfect accuracy.

'In my experience, most people start off puppeteering,
then go to scripting because of its flexibility, then go back
to puppeteering because of its immediacy.'

HUGH HANCOCK, *Machinimator*

Two different approaches to
filming battle scenes: in Ken Thain's
futuristic **The Everseason** (2004,
LEFT), filmed in **Matinee**, every one
of the combatants is scripted,
while in World War II drama **Ours
Again** (2004, ABOVE), from Mu
Productions, they are all played
by real people.

TECHNIQUES 1: AI

Creating machinima can be as easy as pressing the V button on your keyboard. The latest instalment in EA's multi-million dollar blockbuster *The Sims* comes with an inbuilt film-making tool. Previous versions of the game allowed players to take photographs of their little electronic families and create photo albums to share with friends. More enterprising players used this technique to build up photonovels, complete with either captions or comic-book style speech bubbles.

Keeping up with 21st-century fashion, *The Sims 2* includes not just a stills camera, but a video camera. More importantly, the game is now fully 3D, so instead of merely peering down onto their Sims from on high, players can move the camera right down into the action with a degree of freedom that many a real cameraman would envy. Just by pressing the V key, the action is recorded exactly as it is happening on the player's screen, but with most of the game interface stripped away.

The greatest advantage of this is that it's so simple. Furthermore, *The Sims* is more or less unique among games in its subject matter. With the exception of games such as the much more adult and less commercially successful *Singles* from German game company Deep Silver, *The Sims* is the only game to buck the trend and focus on suburban domesticity rather

than fantasy or action. If you want your film to feature cooking a barbecue by the pool, going to the gym, or a romantic evening stargazing, and don't want to have to create custom animations and props, *The Sims* is probably your option.

However, creating a *Friends* or a *Beverly Hills 90210* in *The Sims* isn't entirely straightforward. As it stands, *The Sims* film tool is less a tool for creating kitchen sink dramas or sitcoms than a camcorder for shooting a video at a friend's wedding. You can't just play the game, record the action every now and then, and expect to create something that other people will want to watch. The end result will probably be like a home movie – great if you happened to be there, and tedious if you weren't. AIs are, after all, semi-autonomous. You can tell them what you want them to do, and they'll usually more or less do it, but in their own sweet way. They aren't actors or puppets who will take direction. This loss of creative control conditions how you work.

Plotting a story and working to a script is tricky. AIs react to each other as they see fit, not as you want them too. Rooster Teeth solve this problem in *The Strangerhood* by having several identical characters in different emotional states. They can then bring in 'angry Dutch' or 'happy Dutch' as required for each scene to get the right performance.

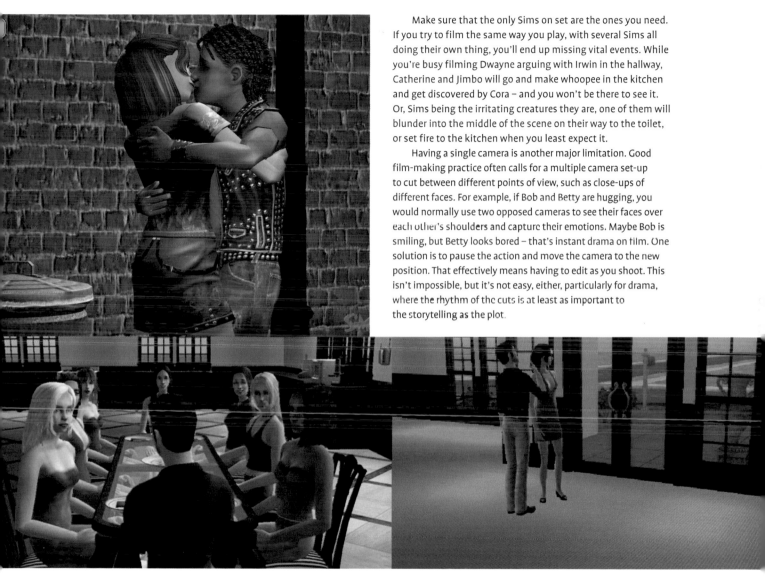

Make sure that the only Sims on set are the ones you need. If you try to film the same way you play, with several Sims all doing their own thing, you'll end up missing vital events. While you're busy filming Dwayne arguing with Irwin in the hallway, Catherine and Jimbo will go and make whoopee in the kitchen and get discovered by Cora – and you won't be there to see it. Or, Sims being the irritating creatures they are, one of them will blunder into the middle of the scene on their way to the toilet, or set fire to the kitchen when you least expect it.

Having a single camera is another major limitation. Good film-making practice often calls for a multiple camera set-up to cut between different points of view, such as close-ups of different faces. For example, if Bob and Betty are hugging, you would normally use two opposed cameras to see their faces over each other's shoulders and capture their emotions. Maybe Bob is smiling, but Betty looks bored – that's instant drama on film. One solution is to pause the action and move the camera to the new position. That effectively means having to edit as you shoot. This isn't impossible, but it's not easy, either, particularly for drama, where the rhythm of the cuts is at least as important to the storytelling as the plot.

TOP ROW: *Your personal **Big Brother** house: **The Sims 2** (2004).*
ABOVE: ***Sim-Ply Reality** (2004) by Artemis Software: one of the first **Sims 2** machinima to appear.*

CASE STUDY: THE MOVIES

The Movies is the latest creation from the stable of gaming legend Peter Molyneux. Nearly three years in development, it is the game that all aspiring machinimators will want when it appears in mid-2005.

On the surface, it's a standard Sim game. You play a movie mogul; you set up a studio, hire actors and directors, build sets, and make films. As the game develops, the art of film-making itself progresses from short black and white silent films to high-tech modern epics.

While the game is entertaining enough, the real joy for machinimators lies in its ability to create films. If you're playing the default simulation mode, you're bound by the limitations of the game in terms of budgets, wardrobe, techniques, and other resources. If you prefer to give free rein to your creativity, you can play in 'sandbox' mode, and everything the game has to offer is open to you.

Creating a film in **The Movies** is both simple and powerful. You can create a five-minute short in around half an hour.

You start by choosing a genre, such as Western, romance, Sci-Fi, horror, or action. You build up the film by selecting a sequence of preset scenes: for example you might use a hold-up in an action film, or an argument in a romance. Next, you select a set for each scene. The game includes several standard sets that you can modify by using various props, such as a diner, an alleyway, or a spaceship control room. You have now created a basic sequence with faceless actors.

Now you select your cast. For each scene, you assign an actor to each role. For example, the holdup scene has A sneaking up behind B with a gun. You could have the hero sneaking up behind your villain, or the villain's henchman sneaking up behind the hero's girlfriend. You have access to a full range of wardrobe and makeup facilities; The Movies boasts well over 500 costumes for male and female characters, each of which you can modify to give it different colours. The makeup ranges from simple eye makeup to all-over body paint and weird alien prosthetics.

This is where the magic of The Movies really kicks in. The basic scenes are only the starting point of the storytelling. You can now modify each scene in various ways using simple slider controls. In the holdup scene, you can control the level of violence and decide whether the assailant simply holds the victim at gunpoint, knocks him to the ground, or savagely breaks his neck. You can add atmospheric effects such as fog or rain, or set the scene at night. You can bring in lights and cameras to get just the shots you want. The action then runs in realtime, and everything works using real physics. If you put a pile of boxes in the street and a character runs into them, they fall to the floor as they should.

When you're happy with the filming, you take the footage into the edit suite, where you produce the final cut. Assign dialogue to a character, and they automatically lip synch to their voice track. You can even change the film stock and go for a period look, such as sepia or Technicolor. The finished film can then be viewed using The Movies or exported as standalone video.

It's simple, it's fun, and it's incredibly versatile. Expansion sets are planned, featuring more costumes, sets, scenes, and genres. Mod kits will enable people to push The Movies in ways the developers, Lionhead, never envisaged.

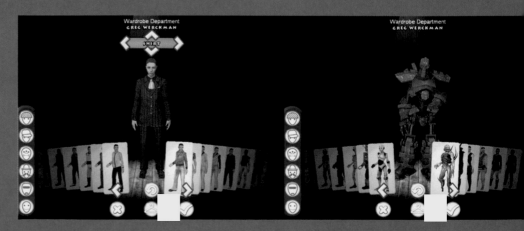

RIGHT: The costume department even allows you to build robots.
FAR RIGHT: Are B-movies set to make a return? Note the way the film is aged to look like 1920s film stock.

TECHNIQUES 2: PUPPETEERING

'I wish I could always use virtual actor puppeteering, since it's the quickest way to generate footage, but you are limited to the actions you predesign into your character. For more dialogue-driven stories it works a lot better, because you just have to figure out the poses that accentuate your dialogue and make sure you can achieve those poses during "game play", but in doing an action film you would need a one-to-one full body motion capture rig to capture the full extent of the necessary character movements.'

KEN THAIN, *Machinimator*

*LEFT: Not quite Russell Crowe or Kirk Douglas, but the arena nevertheless provides a great spectacle: **The Battle of Xerxes** (2003), by Artemis Software.*

*BELOW: **The AVIE Who Shagged Me** (2004), by Munly Leong, is a tour de force of puppeteering. Filmed in **There** with a huge cast, it is a recreation of the second Austin Powers film, complete with dance routines, manic battles, and fembots!*

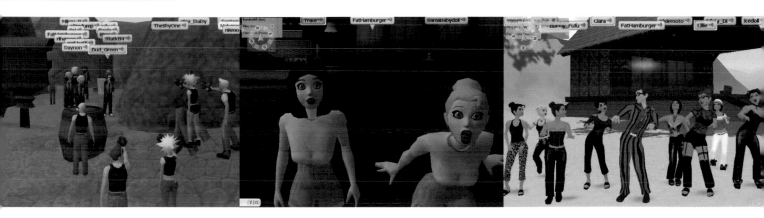

The nearest the machinimator can get to working on a television set or in theatre, rather than computer animation, is to use the game engine as a virtual stage and control each character like a puppet. A cast of puppeteers take a character each, and controls them just as they would in a multiplayer game. Unlike a game, though, these virtual actors have to be trained enough and disciplined enough to hit their marks on cue, move, and speak exactly like real actors. If necessary, the main characters and the humans who are controlling them can be supplemented with extras controlled by AI.

To capture the footage, other crew members are detailed to act as cameramen, or else the director can use the inbuilt cameras provided by the game. While inbuilt cameras are limiting in some ways, they have the advantage that they can run automatically without needing a person to man them, and the number of crew can be kept down.

Each scene and each shot is filmed separately, and the action is recorded to video files. These are then imported into standard video editing software and stitched together to create the final edit.

What makes puppeteering so attractive is its immediacy. Unlike any form of scripted machinima, the results are visible as soon as the shot is taken. A good team of puppeteers can create footage faster than in practically any other medium, and have the flexibility to improvise while they do it. It draws most

heavily on its gameplaying roots, since the puppeteers are using exactly the same interface to act as they would to play a game, albeit in a very different way.

On the other hand, puppeteering is not really a viable option for the solo machinimator. Most stories require more than one character to be on the set at once. While it is possible to control just one character at a time and use AI to control the others, most productions will require several puppeteers. Working with a crew brings its own problems; unless the director is well prepared for the shoot, and knows exactly what he is trying to achieve, it is easy to waste a lot of time for very little return. And, particularly in amateur productions, too much different creative input can lead to ruffled feathers and crews splitting up over 'artistic differences'.

However, if the crew can survive the filming process, puppeteering also lends itself best to benefiting from traditional production processes. Once the footage is recorded, using an offline editor allows machinimators to use exactly the same techniques and tools as film and television directors would, such as dissolves, fades, and colour shifting. Again, this comes at a cost. Video files are usually large, and most of the footage that you film ends up on the cutting-room floor. It is not unreasonable to generate 10GB of video for every minute of finished film, which calls for a substantial amount of hard disk space.

CASE STUDY: A GREAT AND MAJESTIC EMPIRE

A Great and Majestic Empire (AGaME) is a 23-episode comedy series set in the world of *Star Wars*, filmed using the *Jedi Knight* games. It was screened at the Ottawa International Animation Festival in 2004 and was featured on the cover disc of *PC Gamer Magazine*. Producer Denis Cooney, writer Dave Maiden, and actor Dave Gilson, from the group UK Mercs, talk about putting the show together.

Why did you decide to make AGaME?

DG: It was two things that came together. We as a gaming community had been playing *Jedi Knight 2: Jedi Outcast* and *Jedi Knight: Jedi Academy* for a while. However the difference from other players was that we played in a closed server, and really focused on role play rather than who got the most frags. Then we discovered *Red Vs Blue*. They seemed to have a similar subtle way of expressing emotions. I tried making a *JK* video to attract more members of UK Mercs to join us, but Den was the first to really start exploring the storytelling potential of the medium. He made some short proof of concept videos, including one set to the audio track of the Monty Python 'Dead Parrot' sketch.

Do you have any film training or experience?

DM: Apart from playing the second Roman soldier in the school Christmas play, I'd have to say no.

DC: I don't think anyone involved with *AGaME* has any professional film or animation experience at all. But that's half the fun, isn't it? To be able to do something like this and have people enjoy the end product.

How do you go about making the films?

DC: David Maiden or Richard Collins writes a script and sends it over to me. I check it, edit it, then forward it to the other actors. Since several different people do the voices, I often get held up waiting for one of them to finish his lines. It sounds stupid, but since we're not trained actors we all have a fear of recording the lines with other people present. Once the house is empty, recording starts! Once they have recorded their dialogue, I can start filming.

Filming is the easy part. We use *Jedi Knight 2 and 3* from LucasArts for the films. We use special commands to remove the HUD and tweak the default camera. When filming using game

EPISODE
14
'3 PINTS AND A
DONUT PLEASE'

bots I use a sniper rifle's 'zoom' option as a camera. The films are recorded as AVIs using FRAPS, a very cheap and powerful recording package available online.

Then the editing begins. Editing is done in Windows Movie Maker and Premiere. I find it easier to lay the audio track first and add the film clips to fit the scene as best as possible.

How many people are on the crew?
DC: Six in total at the moment; David Maiden and Richard Collins who write the scripts, David Gilson who does the intros and acts, Phil Hetherington and Craig Burton who do voices, and me. On the early episodes I had around eight to ten people working as puppeteers, but trying to control that many people and get them to work instead of shoot each other was a nightmare. Since those who make the film have never met in real life, or even live close together, it's hard to give proper direction. These days the filming is done using game bots and maybe one other puppeteer.

How long does each episode take?
DC: From writing to finished product? I've been able to make an episode in under a week, which I think is incredibly fast. If this were traditional animation that would be nearly unheard of.

DM: Since we all work apart and have our own daily lives to deal with, a few episodes have been known to take a lot longer!

What were you particularly pleased with?
DM: The way the characters are evolving as we go along. One thing I'm always afraid of in any story is that the characters are going to be bland, lifeless, and unidentifiable. This isn't the case with *AGaME*, since the guys have all really got their teeth into the voice characterizations and have given them all a breath of life that you just can't create on paper. Sure, there are some episodes where I think to myself 'I should have done that scene this way', or 'I could have made that funnier'. But anyone who has written anything will always be doing the same thing.

DG: I'm really pleased with how we've been received by the *Star Wars* community of fans.

DM: The last time I checked the website, we had something like 17,000 hits, and I was very happy with that. I still have the bump on my head from when I jumped out of my chair!

DC: I really didn't expect to make a show that was liked or that would last as long as it has. I still get fan mail after nearly a year.

TECHNIQUES 3: RECAMMING

Where machinima becomes almost unique as a creative medium is in the use of a suite of techniques loosely grouped under the term 'recamming'. Some machinima purists insist that recamming is a specific technique developed for *Quake* demos but the underlying principles have much wider application.

Initially, the machinimator uses the puppeteering technique as before, but instead of capturing the footage as a video file, it is recorded in the engine's native demo file format and can be played back and viewed through the original game engine or exported to video.

The difference seems slight until you begin to examine the capabilities of the demo format in detail. While video, once recorded, is forever fixed, demos are continually open to manipulation. It is the equivalent of being able to change the script of a play, and knowing that at the next performance, the actors will deliver the revised version, complete with new lines, new stage directions, and even the scenes in a different order. This is a level of flexibility that no other form of film-making can offer.

A machinimator working with a small team of actors, or even solo, can create a large cast of puppeteered characters, adding them into the scene in successive takes. When the first characters have been recorded, the machinimator plays back the scene, this time controlling and recording a second group of characters. Getting the two takes to interact convincingly requires forethought and practice. However, this is where the greatest strength of this technique comes into play. The machinimator can change the characters' animation tracks, amending the placement or the timing, rather like a theatre director being able to tell an actress, 'Jane, you should have arrived at the doorway slightly earlier'.

Cameras can be added at any time in the process, either fixed or moving. The director can play the action backwards and forwards, in slow motion or at high speed, to choose the optimum camera placement. This divorce between the action and the filming requires careful planning. The machinimator has to create action that will look good from a camera angle he cannot yet see, and be aware of the final composition.

This is made still more complex by the ability to change the lighting at any time. Once the director has chosen the best camera angle to show the action, the set will often need relighting in order to show the characters and sets at their best. In traditional filming, lights and cameras are set up simultaneously; once the director knows more or less where he intends to shoot from, the lights are rigged for that angle, and the director is then committed to that direction. In machinima, the director can choose to move the camera to a totally different part of the set and completely rerig the lights without needing to rerecord the action.

Possibly the most powerful feature of all is the ability to replace whole elements of the sequence. For example, a plain brick wall could be replaced by a shop front, or a plain wooden table turned into a mahogany antique. A clear blue sky could be turned into a stunning sunset, or a dingy cavern turned into an underground Atlantean temple. Even more radically, Jake the musclebound space marine, could be switched for winsome explorer Janine, just by changing the character model.

Although a great fan of raw puppeteering, Ken Thain extols the virtues of using recamming techniques. 'If I decide I want to change the look of my main character totally, I update the skin graphic for that character and then instantly the next time I play back that film, the new character is in. Using puppeteering, I would have to recapture all my footage that has this character, replace the edits in *Premiere* with the new footage, re-export to file and I would be done. This would take more than just a few hours, and most likely days. This is really evolutionary film-making.'

The biggest drawback to using these hybrid techniques is that so few engines support them, and there are few tools. *KeyGrip* works for *Quake 1* and *2*, while Fountainhead's *Machinimation* is based on *Quake 3 Arena*, and is promised for *Doom 3*.

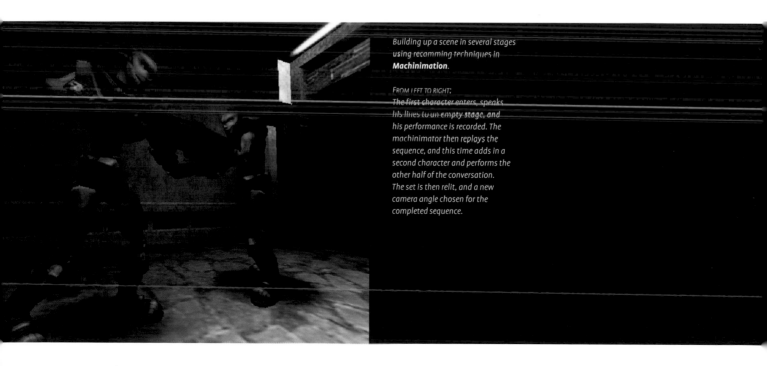

Building up a scene in several stages using recamming techniques in **Machinimation**.

FROM LEFT TO RIGHT:
The first character enters, speaks his lines to an empty stage, and his performance is recorded. The machinimator then replays the sequence, and this time adds in a second character and performs the other half of the conversation. The set is then relit, and a new camera angle chosen for the completed sequence.

CASE STUDY: FOUNTAINHEAD

Fountainhead Entertainment, based in Mesquite, Texas, was founded in 2000 by Katherine Anna Kang, formerly business development director of Id Software. In addition to producing traditional animation, the company developed *Machinimation*, the first commercial-grade tool for machinima, based on Id's *Quake 3 Arena* engine. Fountainhead's machinima creations include the award-winning *Anna* and *In the Waiting Line*, as well as segments of the UPN television show *Game Over*, the first-ever CGI television series developed for primetime. Kang speaks about Fountainhead's experiences with creating machinima.

Can machinima ever compete with traditional animation?
It's possible for machinima to compete with traditional animation but not when there's such a difference in budget. If machinima productions were given even half the budget of traditional animation, I believe machinima would kick butt. It's currently seen as a hobby because it is budgeted as such – meaning, there's usually no budget to speak of.

What makes a good machinima movie?
Any good movie has to have good writing. Good writing, be it a comedy, tragedy, or drama is the foundation necessary to create a great piece. No great work has mediocre writing.

***Machinimation* is very different from *Matinee*, in that it uses puppeteering rather than scripting for the base performances. How does this affect the final film?**
Machinimation creates a more theatre-like atmosphere where performances are just as important as the animation. It allows for spontaneity and slightly different nuances in performances that would not happen in scripted scenes. Overall, I think a combination of the two is ideal.

The biggest limitation of machinima is probably the lack of expression in the characters.
CGI has those problems as well and it's not something that will be fixed anytime in the near future. Those problems virtually disappear when the characters are abstract or not human (i.e. toys, robots, toons, etc.). When we deal with human characters, we're too familiar with the nuances of movement so if they're even slightly off, it takes away from the realism. The fact is that most animation contains stylized characters, whether it's

anime, cartoons, or CGI. I don't believe the facial expression and body language is a problem that can easily be fixed without a huge budget, advanced technology, and a lot of time. Even *Final Fantasy* didn't get it right.

How much are the prospects for commercial machinima hampered by the copyright situation with game engines?
I don't believe that commercial machinima is hampered by copyrights, primarily because of the availability of the *Quake 1* and *Quake 2* engines. The source is free to anyone who wants to utilize it, be it commercial or for non-profit. The only caveat is that they release the source developed on top of the engines and that they create their own art if they choose to take it commercially. Licensing is an option if you choose to do neither. The main thing that seems to 'hamper' the progress is the desire to work with the next greatest and advanced engines, which are available through licensing for commercial use. It's extremely tempting to leave behind older engines and move on to the newer ones. We plan to create a machinima tool that uses a newer engine.

How and why has your approach to machinima changed over the last few years?
Rather than focusing on epics, we focus on smaller pieces and work with what we have. Funding for machinima is non-existent so our approach is to take small steps and chip away at goals rather than plan huge projects in need of funding. Focusing on larger productions ends up taking away from the original goal, which is to make machinima. You spend a lot of time trying to get the tools that you need, such as funding, staff, sales and marketing, and so on.

*RIGHT ABOVE: **In the Waiting Line** (2003).*
*RIGHT BELOW: **Anna** (2003).*

Although hybrid techniques involving both puppeteering and scripting are comparatively rare, pure scripting is becoming increasingly common. More akin to traditional animation than other forms of machinima, the rise of scripted machinima is largely due to the success of *Unreal Tournament 2004* and its accompanying machinima tool, *Matinee*.

Fully scripting machinima sequences is the technique most used by games companies to create cut-scenes. It works just like the recamming techniques discussed earlier, except that the initial puppeteering of the characters is replaced completely with scripts. Each character is given a series of points to move to, and timings for their movements. Every gesture, every head movement, and every change of posture or expression is likewise scripted.

This allows for extreme precision in the control of the characters. Game characters are generally designed for fast, furious activity, rather than the ability to hit their marks on cue. Typically, they have two movement speeds, a walk and a run. Unlike real actors, they can't walk a bit faster or a bit slower to get their timing spot on. Scripting the action means that they will start moving at exactly the right frame, and arrive at exactly the right frame.

It also allows the machinimator to get the best performance from the characters. A typical game interface is focused on movement, inventory control, and combat. For example, game designers don't generally include keyboard commands for controlling facial expressions. By going directly to the script, the machinimator can control not only the facial expression, but the degree of that expression to use.

Matinee provides unparalleled precision in the control of the cameras. They not only move, but roll, pitch, yaw, blur, and shake. The field of view can be changed allowing the machinimator to simulate different lenses.

By carefully adjusting each element in the scene, the machinimator gradually builds up the film, refining each part of the sequence until he achieves the desired result.

However, using scripts to control characters to this degree of precision is slow and laborious. The performance of each character has to be created one at a time, since it is not possible to use a cast of actors performing simultaneously. As a result, fully scripted machinima tends to be much more suited to solo machinimators than groups. Although several people may work on the project, some providing 3D models and others providing sounds, for example, the actual creative process is largely a solitary pursuit.

Using scripts also loses much of the immediacy of puppeteering. In some sense, it is equivalent to the difference between filming marionettes on strings in Gerry Anderson style, or wireframe puppets in stop motion. The puppeteer machinimator can see the results as they happen, and with a good crew can get a finished performance recorded in the time it takes to run through it a few times. The scripter has to input every little element manually, and each time, wait until the film is played back before he can see what he's got and whether he's satisfied with it. While the wait is negligible in comparison with conventional animation, it nevertheless requires a different degree of patience.

RIGHT ABOVE: Julien Vanhoenacker's disturbing and macabre piece **Anthem** *(2003).*
RIGHT: **Cancers** *(2004), by Eric Bakutis, was a finalist in the 2004 Make Something Unreal Contest.*

'Making your first film in a videogame engine is going to take a lot more time than you think it will.'

ERIC BAKUTIS, *Machinimator*

USING GAME ASSETS

One reason why machinima is so easy for first time film-makers to use is that unlike a 3D animation package, the basic game provides everything you need in terms of assets: sets, characters, animations, and sounds. You can create entertaining films without ever having to touch a 3D package or a level editor.

However, while the ingame assets provide plenty to play with, it can get somewhat restricting. After a while, telling the same sort of stories about the same few characters eventually becomes tedious for both the film-maker and the viewer.

The easiest solution is often to use one of the mods already created for a game. Instead of filming in the standard version of *Unreal Tournament 2004*, why not create a film using the *Air Buccaneers* mod? Or the *Dead Cities* mod for *Battlefield 1942*? It'll look very different to the base games, and will enable you to tell new and different stories.

To create truly new and original work, you need to create your own assets. These can be simple changes at first, depending on your skill. You could change the set design by using new textures or meshes, eventually working your way up to building complete new sets. If you're not comfortable with building 3D models of people from scratch, you could adapt an existing model and change the colour of his costume, lengthen his coat, or replace his face.

The more assets that you create, the more original and unique your work will be. Films such as *Scrap*, *Sparked Memory*, *Battle of Xerxes*, and *Eschaton* stand out because they don't look anything like the games that they are based upon. But this originality comes at a price. Building 3D assets takes a lot of time and skill, particularly if you want to achieve the level of quality that can be seen in modern games. This takes

considerable commitment; think carefully about how long you're prepared to spend patiently creating assets before you get on with the actual filming.

'The common misconception regarding machinima production is that creating original productions is also quick and easy,' says Paul Marino. 'While there are great advances being made in the various pieces of modelling and animation software, production is still production, and it usually requires focused resources and time to get the job done right. In this respect, machinima production looks exactly like game asset development – conceptualization, modelling, animation, level design, and texture development. With this in mind, the production time really expands, but the legal headaches are reigned in. In reality, it's all about where you want to balance your time.'

'On *Ours Again*, I built the map using *Battlecraft 1942*, which uses existing in-game assets. No original animations, objects, or anything. The only thing really added to the image was the colour correction/modifications I made to the video footage, which aren't even that unique since I basically ripped off *Saving Private Ryan* and *Band of Brothers* for it.'

NATHAN MOLLER, *Machinimator*

'The true definition of a good machinima team is one that can create an entire movie from scratch and only uses the game engine as their stage.'

ATUSSA SIMON, *Machinimator*

*Machinima that use unmodified games: Phatcorns' **Out for Blood** (2003, ABOVE), created in **Halo**, and **Ours Again** (2004, LEFT), by Mu Productions, created in **Battlefield 1942**.*

COPYRIGHT

The biggest drawback with using in-game assets is the issue of copyright. While most games companies don't mind fans creating machinima films based on their work, some do.

Games industry lawyer Vincent Scheurer of Sarrazin explains. 'If you infringe copyright – even in a way that you think is minor – then it's Armageddon. Copyright is an intellectual property right. Our entire capitalist system is based on the inviolability of our property rights. If X sells a product that infringes Y's copyright, then Y can have every copy of that product taken out of the market and destroyed, and sue for damages as well, no matter how innocent X was, and how expensive these actions might be for X. Some forms of deliberate infringement can land the infringing person in jail for up to 10 years. In reality, accidental infringement hands all the cards to the person whose rights are being infringed – and you don't want to end up in that position.'

Amateur machinima is generally accepted, and it is reasonable to say that any game that comes with mod tools supplied is fair game for amateur machinima. However, a machinima made using characters, sets, and sounds straight out of a game would be considered in law a derivative work, and distributing it commercially without permission would be considered a violation of copyright. Scheurer continues: 'Intellectual property is all about being the only person who can make money out of a particular work. Any person who creates a work will want to be the only person who can benefit financially from that work – and that is essentially what is granted by intellectual property law. Why bother investing millions in a new game if all of your competitors can rip it off as soon as you have shown that it is commercially viable?'

The issue is complex; it is often unclear whether the assets are owned by the game publisher or the developer, or even a third party. 'It all depends on what the developer has to bargain with,' Scheurer points out. 'When the game is being funded by the publisher, the publisher will often insist that it should own the copyright in the game it is funding. In addition, if the game is based on, say, a film licence, which is not owned by either the publisher or the developer, then the licensor, such as the film studio, will often insist on owning copyright in the game just to make sure that it holds on to any new manifestation of its existing intellectual property. It's a case of the Golden Rule of commerce – he who has all the gold makes all the rules! However, it is important to note that a game is made up of a lot of different components that are separate copyright works in their own right. These separate works may, and often do, have separate owners. So one person could own copyright in the music, another person could own it in the text, another could own copyright in the graphics, and yet another person could own it in the underlying algorithms.'

'Fair use' is a defence often quoted by machinimators. However, as IP expert Professor Lawrence Lessig wryly puts it, in the current climate, fair use equates to the right to hire a lawyer. Scheurer expands on this. 'In general, if your film includes a substantial part of a game – and "substantial" in the

Copyright holders Microsoft are supportive of the way Rooster Teeth used **Halo** *to make* **Red vs Blue** *(1993).*

context of copyright often means very little – then you need the permission of the owner of copyright in the game and all of the components of the game which you are using. The "fair use" provisions were always very limited in scope and have been substantially pared back recently. They tend to protect people who incidentally include copyright works in film, which would not be the case with machinima. You should not rely on these provisions unless you are already very familiar with how they work. Giving credit does not absolve you of the need to obtain the permission of the copyright owner.'

Machinimators should take this seriously, says Hugh Hancock. 'We have not had a situation where a large machinima production has been hit yet, but that is bound to change.' Games companies are beginning to take notice of what's going on. 'Our initial plan with *Red vs Blue* was to fly under the radar and hope Microsoft never noticed us but they contacted us pretty quickly...some time right after episode 2,' says Gus of

Rooster Teeth. Fortunately, Microsoft was supportive, and saw it as an opportunity to promote *Halo*. 'They seem to really like *Red vs Blue* and are really great to work with,' he adds.

The Academy of Machinima Arts & Sciences is working with games companies to try and find a solution that fits all. Anthony Bailey is bullish. 'Ultimately if every game company prices themselves out of the market, there will be a solution from the open source community or from a small software start-up with a machinima focus and their own engine.'

Scheurer's closing advice is stark. 'Check with a lawyer. It is not enough to ask the person who you think might be the copyright owner if it is OK to use his work – even if he says "yes" he might not be in a position to grant permission, in which case the permission will be worthless. The penalties for infringing copyright are so substantial that you cannot afford to take chances. The fact that you acted innocently and in good faith at all times is of little consequence.'

Making a machinima production can require a huge raft of specialist skills. Much like traditional films or animation, the best films are a collaboration between many different people, all working within their area of expertise. That's not to say that you can't make machinima on your own; by carefully choosing your techniques and sticking within your limitations when you design the film, you can create perfectly acceptable work by yourself, and have a lot of fun doing so. If you don't have 3D modelling skills, you can still create films using just the original game assets. If you can't write scripts or tell good stories, do a music video or a stunt video. And if you don't want to work with actors, use *Matinee* or *Machinimation* and play all the parts yourself.

But before you embark on a grand solo adventure, you need to be aware of what you could be letting yourself in for; you're not only the director and producer, but the entire cast, cinematographer, cameraman, story writer, scriptwriter, art director, concept artist, set designer, model-maker, make-up artist, hairstylist, props man, armourer, costumer, set-builder, lighting crew, animator, programmer, special

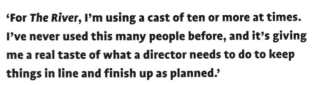

'On *The Journey*, I was alone except for the soundtrack, though I strongly discourage doing those projects on your own. Feedback from a lot of people is essential and the more ideas you have in your production team, the better the movie usually gets.'

FRIEDRICH KIRSCHNER, *Machinimator*

'For *The River*, I'm using a cast of ten or more at times. I've never used this many people before, and it's giving me a real taste of what a director needs to do to keep things in line and finish up as planned.'

IAN KRISTENSEN, *Machinimator*

*LEFT: Political satire in machinima, with **Larry and Lenny on the Campaign Trail** (2003).*
LEFT TO RIGHT: Larry & Lenny giving a campaign speech.
Lenny Lumberjack for President.
The set of '6 Minutes' (3D level design by Vanson Studios).
Larry & Lenny answer questions on the '6 Minutes' news show, with host Mike Whitely.

effects team, sound designer, voice actor, dubber, foley artist, sound engineer, composer, musician, video editor, and video engineer. And you'll probably have to handle all the catering yourself as well. Even great all-rounders such as John Carpenter and Robert Rodriguez would be impressed!

'Unless you're a genius, your overall work is going to suffer if you handle everything by yourself,' advises experienced machinimator Jason Choi. 'Find crew members and split your work.' Letting go of part of the project is one of the hardest things for many people to do. The film that exists in your mind is perfect, and by letting other people have creative input into it, you run the risk of ending up with something that wasn't what you intended, and couldn't possibly be as good. It sometimes

*The ILL Clan, from New York, is one of the most established machinima teams around, and is sufficiently practised that they perform machinima live. Classic comedy in **Common Sense Cooking with Carl the Cook** (2003, ABOVE), by the ILL Clan.*

takes a certain amount of detachment and honesty with yourself to admit that other people's help could be worthwhile.

Machinima teams often collaborate over the Internet, rarely, if ever, meeting in person. Some teams are truly global, with members scattered throughout America, Canada, Australia, and the UK. One person may provide models, another may do some programming, and yet another writes scripts or records music. This can be tricky to organize, but on the other hand, it gives the team great freedom for each person to operate at their own pace and in their own timescales.

ACTORS

The choice of whether to use actors in your crew is very different from the choice of using any other specialists in that it is a technical decision, and not a creative one. If you choose to use the raw puppeteering method, without the benefit of a tool such as *Machinimation* for adding in extra characters, you will need actors unless you're filming a monologue. On the other hand, if you're filming in *Matinee*, you won't need actors, because there is no puppeteering to be done. This, more than anything else, may influence your choice of how to make machinima. If you don't have a cast, you can't puppeteer.

The actor's job is to control a character in a scene. Unlike a real actor, the same person can take many different roles in the same film, or even in different shots in the same scene; one minute, you could be driving hell for leather through an enemy base under fire, and in the next shot, you could be one of those enemies in close-up, blazing away at an offscreen jeep. This allows you to be very efficient about the number of actors you need.

A good machinima actor needs to be able to control an ingame character fluidly and without having to think too hard about it. Although the skills required for acting are

*A large cast is often useful when creating battle scenes, as the Northern Brigade's **The Hero** (2002) demonstrates. The actors have to rehearse working together to create interesting footage, rather than simply play the game.*

different from the skills required to win in an FPS, fluency with keyboard and mouse controls are essential, to the extent that the actor needs to feel that they are in the virtual world, not sitting at a computer controlling an imaginary character. Where the actor differs from the gamer is that this identification with the character needs to be translated into expression. Unless you are making a stunt film, it is not enough to be able to move fast, target quickly, make pixel-perfect jumps, and dodge incoming missiles. The actor needs to be able to use the character's limited body language to create a dramatic performance.

A simple screen test for an actor consists of asking them to walk across a room to a certain point, turn, look back at the camera, and then nod as if agreeing with something being said to them. It's surprising how hard this is. Gamers are used to running, not walking. Hitting a mark when you can't see your feet is tricky. Turning around in a way that looks natural is even harder when you can't control your hips or your shoulders directly. And it takes practice to develop the subtlety to nod gently rather than waggle your head furiously up and down.

Actors also need a sense of discipline. It's easy to forget that you're supposed to be making a film, and find yourself playing games instead, particularly while waiting for a take.

The ideal machinima actor is also a cameraman. The cameras are controlled by players just like the characters, moving to track the action, using techniques such as dollying, crane shots, and rolling. This takes the gamer's skillset and develops it in another direction. The cameraman requires not only a good understanding of how to control the camera smoothly and precisely, but what constitutes a well-framed and well-composed shot, and how to get the shot the director wants.

Often, the cast members in a machinima production are not even in the same place, but log into the virtual world via the Internet, just like when playing games. This raises all sorts of communication issues. Voice chat programs such as *Teamspeak* are popular solutions. 'Once everyone knows your voice on *Teamspeak* they will pipe down while you are directing,' adds Ian 'Pappy Boyington' Kristensen, who specializes in making action films in *Battlefield 1942*. 'I can set the scene up and simply give cues for people to start their actions.'

> **'What makes a good machinima movie? Story.
> It needs a good story – compelling characters,
> interesting plot, twists, good structure, the works.
> That's where many machinima pieces fall down,
> and why I keep banging on about books like Robert
> McKee's *Story Structure* until I'm hoarse.'**
>
> HUGH HANCOCK, *Machinimator*

Most film-making is storytelling. Unless you're making stunt videos or documentaries, the heart of your film is a work of fiction. Without a good story, your audience will quickly lose interest. They need to care about who these people are, why they're doing what they're doing, and why it matters. In E.M. Forster's famous summation, 'The king died and then the queen died', isn't a story. It's a sequence of events. 'The king died and then the queen died of grief.' Now that's a story.

It's an oft-repeated maxim that anyone can tell a story, and everyone's got a book inside them. Maybe so, but not everyone can tell a good story or has an interesting book inside them. The screenwriter's craft is something that has to be learned, honed, and practised. Over the last century, writers have developed ways of telling stories in film that work. They know how to take an audience for a ride, and provoke in them the emotions that they wish to portray. They know how to lull their audiences into a sense of security, and then surprise them or shock them at the right moment for maximum effect.

If the story is compelling enough, the limitations of the medium become less important. Some of the most effective and engrossing stories in the world are the epic myths of Southeast Asia, told with shadow puppets, probably the most limited visual medium of all. Audiences flocked to see *The Blair Witch Project* for its storytelling, not its technical wizardry.

Story creation breaks down into two distinct roles: storywriting and scriptwriting. These are often, but by no means always, done by the same person. Successful TV series like *The X-Files* or *Coronation Street* deliberately split the task; one team oversees the storyline for an entire season, and then individual episodes are written by different scriptwriters.

The storywriter creates the overall plot, the characters, and the themes. This is the area where innovation is required. The story 'some guys get together and rob a bank' is pretty uninspiring, but it's a starting point. But turn that into 'some disgruntled soldiers hear of a cache of stolen gold in a bank behind enemy lines, and, led by a demoted but highly skilled officer and a crazed tank commander, desert, and break through enemy lines to steal the gold' – now you've got the bare bones of *Kelly's Heroes*, a much more interesting concept. The storywriter then fleshes out not only the rest of the story, but also the characters and their relationships. In *Kelly's Heroes*, the power struggle between Telly Savalas, the platoon commander, and Clint Eastwood, the demoted officer, is central to the plot.

The scriptwriter's task is to turn that story into dialogue and basic staging directions. Having decided that the hero is going to be a tough hardbitten gangster, the writer needs to make him speak like one. The line between convincing dialogue and laughable pastiche is often a fine one, as many a straight to video film will attest. Dialogue for film or television is a very specific skill, and nothing like writing dialogue for novels or short stories, or even radio. Phraseology that works in print does not necessarily translate into film.

*LEFT: Strange Company's Lovecraftian **Eschaton: Nightfall**, (1999) made in **Quake 2** and (BELOW) Damien Valentine's take on **Buffy the Vampire Slayer**, **Consanguinity** (2004), made in a modified version of **Neverwinter Nights**, prove that you don't need state-of-the-art graphics to tell an engaging story.*

MODELLERS AND ARTISTS

'This is the first time I've ever modelled, boned, skinned, or animated organic characters in a 3D program. I learned so much stuff in the three months I worked on *Sparked Memory*, that my head is still deflating!'

CSWAT, *Machinimator*

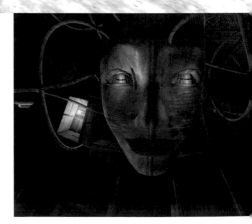

The modelling crew is responsible for creating all the things that will be seen on screen: characters, sets, vehicles, props, even the sky or the distant shimmer of the rings around a far-off planet. They have to take everything in the director's imagination that doesn't already exist in the game and build it in the virtual world.

The task traditionally breaks down into two groups. 2D artists effectively paint flat digital pictures using tools like Adobe Photoshop, while 3D artists build three-dimensional objects with tools including 3D Studio Max or Maya. Some artists specialize in one or the other; some can do both.

The two tasks are thoroughly intertwined. The 3D artist builds geometrical shapes, known as meshes, which he then covers with 2D images, known as textures.

Both 3D and 2D art can be quite daunting for the beginner. Most art software packages are complex and uncompromisingly confusing. However, with the wealth of specialist books, online tutorials, and the help of user groups on the Net, acquiring basic familiarity with the tools is simply a matter of perseverance.

If you don't feel like creating models from scratch, there are easy first steps. Reskinning is comparatively simple. A character in a game usually consists of two parts, the raw 3D model of the character, and a painted 2D 'skin' that is wrapped around it and contains all the colour information. By editing the skin in a 2D painting program, and using that instead of the standard skin, you can create a new character for your film without any 3D modelling skills.

However, until you start changing their body shape, the characters will always look like the originals, in just the same way that Arnold Schwarzenegger will always look like Arnie,

no matter what costume you put him in, or whether he's wearing a wig. To make an actor look really different, you need to use prosthetics. Our virtual actors, however, are less fussy about our making 'permanent' alterations to their bodies, so instead of just sticking latex all over them, you can stretch them, deform them, and even lop bits off them without hearing a word of complaint.

In the machinima environment, modelling and painting talents alone need to be supplemented by other very specific skills. Good concept art speeds up the entire production process. Pencil sketches, usually black and white, enable the model-makers to understand what is wanted, and allow the artists to experiment with different ideas before starting to build on the computer.

Set-building requires a very different approach to designing game levels. The challenge for the machinima set-builder is to create an interesting environment for the characters to perform in, not to create a hostile environment for players to fight in. Some tools allow set-builders to create sets without needing to create 3D models from scratch. Starting with a landscape, stock items such as trees or rivers can be dropped in and moved around rather like building a toy farm. Lighting the set is the final part of the task. Lighting not only creates atmosphere, but is used to highlight the action and draw the viewer's eye to the right place on the screen. Just as lighting for film, video, and stage requires different techniques to bring out the best in the medium, lighting for machinima also requires careful attention in order to work as well as possible with the textures and the shadowing capability of the engine.

*ALL IMAGES: **Bot** (2004), by Digital Yolk, boasts some of the finest models and sets of any machinima to date.*

ANIMATORS

Models are all very well, but films are motion pictures. They have to move. The more movement there is on the screen, the more the audience believes in the reality of what they are seeing. The animator's art is to be the Doctor Frankenstein of the team: to breathe life into the motionless, expressionless golems created by the modellers.

Where the machinima animator and the game animator differ from the traditional animator is that they have to create a character that can be operated interactively in realtime. The traditional animator painstakingly builds a custom animation sequence for each shot, but the game animator has to create a library of animations that can be called on at any time. To make the movement more convincing, the character has to be able to transition seamlessly between the different animations; from running to crouching, crawling, or jumping, for example. To make matters still more complex, a given character may need to be doing several different things simultaneously: running while reloading a weapon, turning his head to look around, and shouting to a comrade.

*Bottom: **Killer Robot** (2003), by Nanoflix, is entirely created from custom animations.*
*Below: Oliver Bermes' **The Infiltrators** (2004) is packed with simple but effective custom animations. In this example,* the lead character sinks to his knees, smashes open a door, and wipes his forehead. Touches such as these differentiate this level of machinima from films made using only the animations created for the games.

'Computer and platform games put much of the animation control in the hands of gamers. This poses the challenge to create great animation that works regardless of what move the gamer decides to make. Games are a combination of user-controlled animation and preset/narrative animation.'

ISAAC KERLOW, *The Art of 3D*

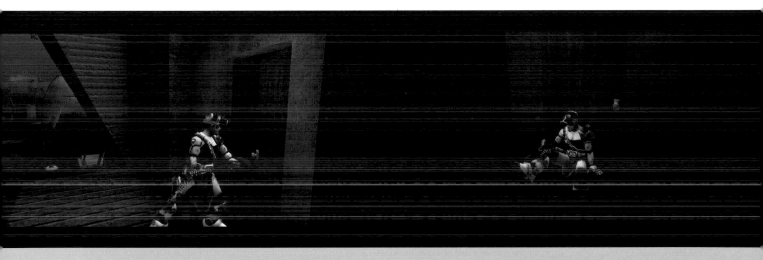

The game animator does not achieve this by creating a specific animation for each possible combination or sequence of actions. This would create a combinatorial explosion of animations that would be beyond the scope of even the largest development team. Instead, they use a system of animation blending. Several different animations are combined to produce a single character; running legs, a standard torso, arms and a weapon performing a reload sequence, a twisting head, and a facial expression.

The game animator has further flexibility by using skeletal animation. Instead of animating each actual character, the animator works with a skeleton and defines a generic movement for a particular skeleton type. For example, a goblin might jump in a particular way, or have a distinctive way of scuttling towards an enemy. The animator can then apply the same animation to a different creature, and it will move like the goblin. Even if the body is a different shape, the motion will be the same.

And it's not just living things that need animation. Vehicles, weapons, and other machines all move. Even smoke, flames, and water move. Grass and leaves sway. Saloon signs creak slowly back and forth. It is the tiny details that transform machinima from mere puppetry to a truly filmic experience.

If this sounds like a mammoth task, it is. 'Poor animation instills life in everything that is dead, but conversely, it deadens everything that is alive,' comments Ubisoft's lead animator Gilles Monteil in an interview for *Develop* magazine, speaking about the animation on their recent title *Splinter Cell: Chaos Theory*. 'It's not simple to do – it's an enormous amount of development work, and it took us an awful lot of time to get where we did, but it was worth it.'

PROGRAMMERS

Programming allows machinimators to get down and dirty with the underlying game engine. This means they can push the game engine past the limits of the original game. More than anything, this is what distinguishes machinima from other forms of film-making. Animators use their tools to create their films. Machinimators often have to make theirs from scratch. If you want to do more than use the basic game engine, the chances are you'll have to do some coding.

Some elementary programming knowledge is often required just to import new characters and other models into the game. Simply to add a new vehicle to *Battlefield 1942*, you need to plug in not just the model, textures, and animations, but all the sounds for it to move, fire, or explode, the physics to define how it handles, data about its weapons, armour, and ammunition, rules for having multiple people in the vehicle, and so on. This work requires a considerable familiarity with the game engine.

For some of the spectacular action sequences in Short Fuze's *No Licence*, effects director Matt Stone built a custom weapon for *Battlefield 1942*, called the explodamatic. This

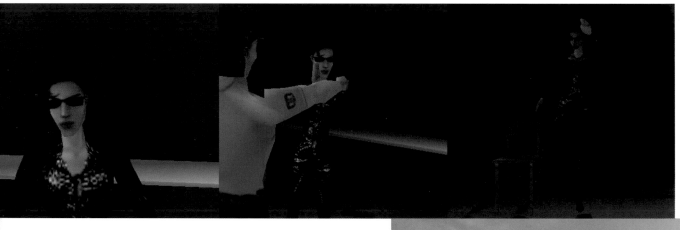

'Machinima is currently totally fragmented and everyone creates his own tool sets again and again. This is like many craftsmen using different models of a hammer. So every tool and technique that can be used for more than one game, something like FRAPS or video encoding in general, is very welcome.'

UWE GIRLICH, *Machinima tool developer*

*ABOVE: The engine for Alexander Jhin's **Sims Matrix** (2004) was programmed from scratch, using character models from **The Sims**. RIGHT: Eric Bakutis developed his own lip synch technology for **Cancers** (2004).*

long-range, rapid-fire gun fired rounds that produced enormous explosions but did practically no damage. For the closing sequence, where an airfield is destroyed, several members of the effects team, armed with explodamatics, stood out of camera shot firing onto the set, creating a huge fiery backdrop to the action.

Where programming goes beyond just game modding is in the specialist machinima tools. One of the most important areas of development is lip synching. Game characters have little need for accurate lip synch, but many animators regard it as essential. 'The lip synching in *Cancers* is my own creation,' says Eric Bakutis. His custom code for *Unreal Tournament 2004* uses a selection of facial textures to represent different lip positions for the different phonemes, or sounds. 'The code parses a string passed from a scripted action that tells it what phonemes to play in what order, so lip synching each line is as simple as isolating the predominant sounds in each 0.2 seconds of the line and entering the phoneme. The string "face", for example, plays the F phoneme, the A phoneme, the C phoneme, and the E phoneme, before reverting to the default head skin.'

This approach to facial animation is based on the classic animator's concept of visemes, popularized by Disney. There are several distinctive mouth positions; Disney use 12, lip-readers recognize 18. The lip synch needs to analyse which of the mouth positions is appropriate and move the character's face accordingly. The major advantage of using visemes is that one viseme works for several different phonemes, so you need fewer of them.

Strange Company's *TOGLFaceS* (Take Over GL Face Skins) utility provides similar functionality for *Neverwinter Nights*. 'By intercepting the Open GL instructions that the engine uses to draw images to the screen on the machine acting as the camera, and changing some of them in realtime, we can overlay new and animated faces on top of the static ones the engine produces,' explains programmer Anthony Bailey. 'By wiring the changes up to various keypresses, we allow someone to "puppet" the mouth and facial expressions of characters as they appear in the captured video frames, controlling them live at the same time that the scenes are acted out and shot within the game. There was already a program called *GL Intercept*, written to intercept and record a log of this sort of stream of graphics instructions. Since it was published under an open licence that allows people to build on and modify its source code to make it do new things, that's what I did to make *TOGLFaceS*. The tool is still a work in progress, but I hope it can eventually be generalized to work with other similarly closed engines that render on PCs using Open GL, or DirectX, and that would be good to use for machinima if they weren't missing this important piece of functionality.'

SOUND CREW

Bad sound is the quickest way to ruin a good film. Good sound can make it. Some directors maintain that you should be able to close your eyes, just listen to the film, and still enjoy it. (Others say that if you can do this, it's a radio play with pictures, not a true film. It depends on the director's prejudices.) Many films, particularly music videos, are little more than the visuals to accompany a good soundtrack.

The task of the sound crew breaks down into four main areas: recording the dialogue, foley, and music, and mixing them all together. A good voice actor creates characterization and emotion in dialogue just by the tone, rhythm, and pitch of his or her voice. In Walt Disney's *Aladdin*, the genie, voiced by Robin Williams, was largely responsible for the success of the film. Had the character been voiced by another actor, the genie would have been a completely different character, even with the same visuals, and the film would have been very different.

Using good voice actors is particularly important for machinima. The quality of the actor's performance has to compensate for the comparative woodenness of the character models themselves. If you plan to record the voices at home, you'll need a soundproof area to work, without too many echoes, and a good-quality microphone, or else everything you record will sound thin and flat. Some music outboard gear would also be a great advantage – a good reverb unit is essential, and a compressor, parametric EQ, chorus, or aural exciter can also juice things up.

Foley is all the sounds that make the environment feel real. The game engine can usually provide enough of this automatically, but you can achieve greater individuality by adding in your own sounds. These include basic sounds such as footsteps, doors opening and closing, and vehicle engines, as well as atmospherics such as birdsong, traffic, or gently lapping waves on a seashore, and special effects such as explosions or whirring spaceships. The amateur can usually get away with using foley sounds from a sound-effects library, which are easily available at a fairly low cost.

A professional foley studio contains a range of different surfaces to produce different footstep effects, as well as variety of specialized noisemakers. Foley artists act out the onscreen action; by pacing cautiously, rather than confidently, a skilled foley artist can make a simple walk appear more slow and measured than it actually is. Adding the swish of trouser legs or the muffled clinking of coins in a pocket to the basic footsteps makes the walk seem different again. In one unforgettable scene in Kurosawa's masterpiece *Throne of Blood*, the only sound is the eerie rustling of a silk kimono as the villainess walks slowly across the screen. It is a supreme example of what good foley work can achieve. The aim of the foley artist is not to create sounds that are accurate, but sounds that work well on screen. Note the way that cars in films routinely screech to a halt or squeal as they pull away, without any trace of skidding or wheelspin. Why? Because it just sounds better.

ABOVE: Scott Buckley's ethereal music for Folklore's **Scrap** (2004) is highly reminiscent of Danny Elfman's score for **Edward Scissorhands** and other Tim Burton big-screen fantasies.

FAR LEFT: A typical home sound studio setup.

LEFT: A professional sound studio, belonging to London's Earcom.

Music is the final element in the sound composition. Before films had sound, they had music, whether it was just piano, or a full orchestra. Lifting music from CDs is common but almost certainly constitutes a copyright violation. Specially composed music makes works like Scrap, Bot, and The Journey stand out.

Sound production is completed by mixing together the dialogue, the foley, and the music. The sound engineer has to focus initially on getting the volume levels right. Music or sound effects must not be allowed to obscure the dialogue, unless this is important for the drama. Sounds also need to be placed at the right point in the stereo or the surround mix, so that they appear to be coming from the right place. And finally, the engineer has to make sure that the ambience of all the sounds match. If the dialogue sounds as if it's recorded in a cathedral, while the footsteps sound like a garage, the audience will immediately sense that something is wrong, even if they can't place exactly what it is.

VIDEO EDITORS AND ENGINEERS

Unless you're working exclusively in a specialist machinima environment such as *Matinee* or *Machinimation*, your final film will be assembled and mastered using non-linear video editing software. This allows you to cut together the different shots you've taken, and choose the best takes that you got.

Editing is what creates the rhythm of a film. However interesting the action, watching from the same camera angle rapidly becomes tedious. Cutting between different cameras keeps viewers interested by constantly refocusing on what the director wants them to see. A segment which cuts rarely feels slow and languid, while a segment that cuts frequently feels exciting. In intense action sequences, cutting every second is quite normal. Much of the effect is achieved by throwing away frames, shots, or whole scenes in order to keep the film moving. This requires a certain degree of ruthlessness when a shot that has taken hours to create is summarily dumped.

The benefit of editing in a non-linear video editing suite rather than in the game engine is that it offers much more flexibility. You can superimpose several different layers of film to create complex special effects. You can use blue screen techniques to add in views through windows or binocular views. By far the most important benefit, though, is the control of transitions. The commonest is the dissolve, where one segment of film gradually gives way to another. Using a video editing

suite, this is simple. The two segments of film are overlapped, and the software will smoothly dissolve from one into the other.

The editor's greatest skill is to create scenes that didn't actually happen on set. For example, if someone turns to look behind him, and you then show a shot of a group of ninjas creeping towards the camera, the audience assumes that the ninjas are actually creeping up behind him. In practice, you could have filmed the ninjas on a different day, or even in a different set; they could even have been intended for a different scene. The editor makes it look seamless and as though that was what the director intended all along.

The video editor can also create special effects at this stage. In *No Licence*, video editor Phil South enhanced the explosion sequences by adding in flash frames. These are single frames of pure white that make the explosions look more dramatic than they were when recorded. The viewer's eyes and brain instinctively react with shock at the brief visual overload.

Video editing software is very much a matter of personal choice, and many people prefer to use Macs rather than PCs. Both platforms provide entry level applications with basic functionality: Moviemaker on Windows XP, and iMovie on the Mac. The main professional quality applications are Adobe Premiere and Final Cut Pro, both of which provide the home machinimator with the ability to create films to broadcast

LEFT: In **The Return** (2004), Ted Brown tells the story of an epic journey quickly and succinctly by cutting rapidly between key incidents to keep up the pace.

ABOVE: The chase scene in Short Fuze's **No Licence** (2004) was made more exciting by using Premiere's matte features to splice two shots together and bring the two vehicles closer together as they hurtle over a cliff. Adding the upper and lower borders to reduce the aspect ratio from 4:3 to 16:9 tightens the viewer's focus on the action.

television standard. Both these tools can be expanded with add-on software, such as Adobe After Effects, or Apple Shake, which provide additional digital effects capability.

The final stage of your film will be mastering it and preparing it for distribution. The video files need to be turned into suitable format for DVD or Web release. To do this, you need to know your way around video codecs (coder/decoders). These compress the files so that they can be downloaded quickly or will fit onto a disc.

DIRECTOR/PRODUCER

The main reason most people choose to make machinima is that they can shoot straight for the top jobs. With no star actors to take top billing, the director and producer can take all of the glory. Everyone wants to be a Lucas or a Spielberg, not a Russell Carpenter or a Conrad Buff, however valuable their contributions are.

Most machinima productions are small enough that the jobs of director and producer are combined. The producer's role is essentially one of management, making sure that the team has everything they need to do their jobs, and ensuring that the production remains on time and on budget. The director's role is to be the lead creative force. While the director does not need to be able to do everyone else's job for them, and should usually be discouraged from doing so, he needs to understand exactly what it is they do, and work with them to get the best from them.

Directing is undoubtedly the most rewarding part of the entire creative process, but it is also the most demanding. The popular image of the film director is the person sitting on a chair with a megaphone telling the actors what to do, and peering through camera lenses telling the cameramen where to point their cameras. Nothing could be further from the truth. Shooting the film is the fun and glamorous part of the job. As director, you will have to supervise every stage of production, from script to storyboard, modelling, camera placement, and staging, right through to editing, sound, music, and even putting the credits on. When filming starts, a good director has already done so much preparation that the shoot should run like

clockwork. And when filming is over and the actors move onto the next job, the director returns to his darkened room with his reels of footage to collaborate with the editor on the slow and painful process of assembling the film.

There are many different styles of director. Some are notoriously tyrannical and perfectionist. Others are more easygoing, and like to take input from their cast and crew at all levels. Both can achieve stunning results, but it's worth remembering that in an amateur production, if you treat your volunteers badly, you may well find yourself with an uncompleted film, and several friends poorer. Your powers of cajoling and persuasion are as important to a successful production as your understanding of how to shoot an exciting action scene. But in the end, it's the passion that you bring to the film as director that will stand out above anything else.

Combining the role of director and producer requires a great deal of discipline. In many ways, the producer's job is very negative. It is the producer's thankless task to tell the director what he can't do, and to keep spurring him on until he finishes the piece. Directors have grand ambitions for their projects, frequently overreaching their ability. As a result, the two are often in conflict; the director wants to spend more time on a particular scene, but the producer wants to wrap it and move on. The director has a great idea for a shot, but this will involve building a huge set that will take weeks. The producer says it isn't worth the extra effort. Sometimes your hardest task will be to release a film knowing you could have done it better if only you'd put in more time and effort.

*OPPOSITE PAGE: When making the music video **Rebel vs Thug** (2003), director/producer Ken Thain had to make hard choices between what he wanted to do creatively as director, and the need to deliver a finished film on time to fit his client's release schedule.*

*In addition to directing and producing their own films, machinimators like Nathan Moller, who created **Ours Again** (BOTTOM), and Eric Bakutis, who created **Cancers** (BELOW), contribute in various ways to other directors' films.*

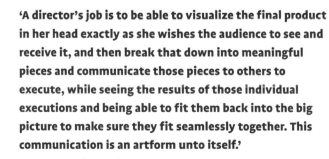

'A director's job is to be able to visualize the final product in her head exactly as she wishes the audience to see and receive it, and then break that down into meaningful pieces and communicate those pieces to others to execute, while seeing the results of those individual executions and being able to fit them back into the big picture to make sure they fit seamlessly together. This communication is an artform unto itself.'

INGRID MOON, *film-maker*

THE MACHINIMA STUDIO

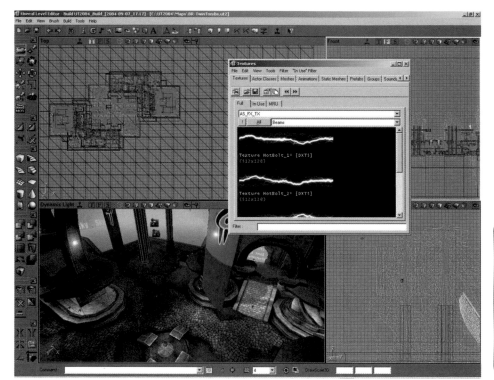

LEFT: **UnrealEd** is the editing tool for Unreal Tournament.
BELOW: **FRAPS** is essential for capturing the action while puppeteering.
RIGHT: **Nero** allows you to burn your valuable files onto DVD-ROM for safekeeping.

Setting up a studio to make machinima depends entirely on the techniques to be employed and what exactly the machinimator intends to create. Machinima can be made on the family computer or can involve a rack of dedicated computers networked together and running a stack of specialist software.

The heart of the entire operation is a good-quality PC to run the game. Some machinima, such as *Red vs Blue*, are still made using Xbox consoles, but this is increasingly rare. As a rule, to make machinima, you need a PC that surpasses the game manufacturer's recommended specifications, and that runs the game smoothly at the highest resolution with all the options turned on. This varies from game to game, so check the specification for your chosen engine. System requirements are increasing all the time, so a PC two years old will be unlikely to do justice to the very latest games.

If the video footage is captured with FRAPS, this puts an additional strain on the game PC; it is wise to allow at least 256MB of additional memory and invest in a second hard disk in order to ensure that the captured footage is smooth. In addition, plenty of disk space for storing video files is essential; particularly when several cameras are employed simultaneously. Each camera can take up to 25MB of video per second, so huge files are common. It is highly advisable to invest in some way of archiving and backing up those irreplaceable files. There are many options to choose from; most common are a DVD-ROM burner or a tape drive.

For a team to work together, a game server is usually required. There are public servers available for most games, but these are frequently crowded, and it is hard to film while there are people wandering around. The alternative is to set up a private server and only allow your cast and crew to use it. Often this can be done with the same PC you are using to perform or act if it is powerful enough, but an alternative is to set aside a separate PC as the server.

BELOW: *Photoshop is the 2D art package of choice, and is ideal for creating title graphics as well as character skins.*
BOTTOM: **Machinimation** *allows you to create machinima using the* **Quake 3 Arena** *engine.*

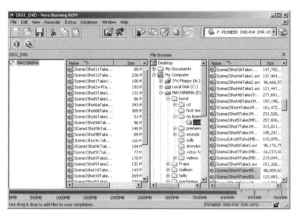

'**Back up everything, every 30 minutes or so. Be extra paranoid and keep backups of your backups. Trust me, everything that can go wrong, absolutely will go wrong. And when it happens, you're probably going to want to take a sledgehammer to your computer.**'

JASON CHOI, *Machinimator*

A team of puppeteers working online needs some way to communicate effectively. Headsets and mikes are far more effective than typing, particularly when shooting. Microphones, and appropriate soundproofing, are also vital for recording dialogue. It works best if everyone has broadband to minimize ping times – although you can work over slower speeds, lag can ruin an otherwise great take.

If everyone in the team is working in the same room, do not underestimate the amount of space required to fit in desks, chairs, and cups of coffee! A large central monitor so that everyone can see the footage can save a lot of pushing and shoving. The room in which shooting is taking place can get very noisy and frenetic. It is often a good idea to provide a smaller, separate quiet room in which the editor can put together rough cuts and archive the footage without too much interference, and somewhere else for unoccupied members of the crew to go to relax while others are working.

MACHINIMA ENGINES

The single most important decision for the machinimator is which game engine to use. Most simply stick with their favourite games. For fan films and stunt films set in the original game world, this is an obvious decision.

For machinima that breaks away from the base game, on the other hand, the choice of engine defines what can be done, what tools will be needed, how many crew will be needed, and what techniques can be employed. If the film will employ mostly game assets, the choice of engine defines what sets, characters, and animations can be used in the story. If the film will use custom assets, there must be some kind of mod tools available for it so that they can be imported. Before choosing an engine, it is well worth looking into the mod community to see what can be done with it, and how flexible it really is.

Battlefield 1942 and *Unreal Tournament 2004*, for example, are immensely flexible engines that lend themselves to all sorts of tinkering. It is vital to evaluate the engine in terms of its potential as a virtual film set, not in terms of its basic gameplay. Films such as *Scrap* owe next to nothing to the gameplay elements of *UT2004*; the use of *Matinee* to create this film has nothing to do with using the engine to create multiplayer carnage in a futuristic world.

A selection of machinima made in unusual engines.
*BELOW LEFT: **Killer Robot** (2003), by Nanoflix, filmed in **GameStudio**.*
*BELOW: Strange Company's **Bloodspell** (2005) uses **Neverwinter Nights**, by Bioware.*

*ABOVE: Artemis Software's **Nesmut** (2004) uses Microsoft's **Age of Mythology**.*

By far the most common type of game engine to use for machinima is the FPS, or first-person shooter. Some diehard machinimators still swear by *Quake 2* and *Quake 3 Arena*, but in terms of graphics and animation quality, these are now beginning to show their age against more modern games. Even old stalwarts such as *Halo* and *Battlefield 1942* are beginning to look tired and clunky compared to their successors *Halo 2* and *Battlefield 2*.

It seems that sequels have the edge when it comes to machinima. Once the developers have created a good basic game, they focus their energies more on the visual quality than the gameplay. Id's *Doom 3* is to all intents and purposes exactly the same game as *Doom*, but much, much better looking. *Half-Life 2* from Valve raises the bar still higher. *Max Payne 2*, by Rockstar, is also becoming popular for gangster films. Crytek's *Far Cry* is one of the new original FPS titles that has been embraced by machinimators.

Massively multiplayer games are also popular machinima engines. They lend themselves to productions with large casts, and the game engines often include a reasonable range of gestures (or emotes) in order to bolster the social side of the game. Popular engines include *EverQuest*, *Second Life*, *City of Heroes*, and *World of Warcraft*. Newer titles such as *Herrcot* have yet to catch on in the mainstream but certainly offer plenty of potential.

More unusual alternatives include *Neverwinter Nights*, *Morrowind*, *Age of Mythology*, *Warhammer 40,000: Dawn of War*, and *Heavy Metal: FAKK2*. These require an enormous amount of creativity and ingenuity to make them work well, but the results are often innovative and surprising.

One of the very few alternatives to running a commercial game to create machinima is *GameStudio*, championed by Peter Rasmussen of Nanoflix. 'GameStudio is a 3D game authoring package. It is open and versatile enough to create pretty much any kind of game. But being so open has meant that I have had to do a great deal of programming myself,' says Rasmussen. 'For *Killer Robot* I developed a system incorporating a conventional animation package called *TrueSpace*, which has sophisticated handling systems for animation, hierarchy, and physics. It uses a scripting language called Python, which is relatively easy to work in. With it I created a routine that writes a frame by frame text record of the animation sequences from *TrueSpace*, which can then be read by a routine I created in the World Definition Language of *GameStudio*.'

THE MACHINIMATOR'S GUIDE

In Norton Juster's classic novel *The Phantom Tollbooth*, Milo undertakes a quest that takes him to some very unusual places. When he returns, he learns the one thing nobody would tell him before he set out: what he had just done was impossible. If he'd known that when he started, he wouldn't have succeeded. There's some truth in that. Ignorance is often a powerful weapon when you're trying something new: with blind faith and determination you can sometimes achieve things that conventional wisdom says can't be done.

On the other hand, learning a new craft is a slow and often painful process. Experimentation and exploration result in dead ends and disasters more often than not. You can learn much from the mistakes of others, as well as building on their successes.

In the closing section of the book, we'll get down to the nitty-gritty of making machinima, pillaging techniques from many other media. We'll also show you some of the possible pitfalls that await the unwary machinimator.

'If I have seen farther, it is by standing on the shoulders of giants.'

ISAAC NEWTON

'Express your own creativity. If you love what you do, others will, too.'

KATHERINE ANNA KANG, *Fountainhead Entertainment*

Halla, by Moppi Productions.

PART 3

THE PRODUCTION PROCESS

Perfect Preparation Prevents Piss-Poor Performance, runs the old army motto. It's as true of film-making as it is of soldiering. The temptation is always to rush straight into filming. After all, it's the exciting bit of making a machinima, and it's so easy to get results straightaway. Unfortunately, it's almost certainly a recipe for disaster.

Film and television – and many other media – work in a tried and trusted method. It requires a certain amount of self-discipline, and it can be very frustrating, but it works, and it will save you time, effort, and heartache in the long run. It's called the production process.

There are three main stages to any production process, and they apply as much to the lowliest machinima as they do to the most expensive film. They are as follows:

PREPRODUCTION

You decide what it is you're going to do, and get everything ready. You figure out the story, write the script, work out what models you need, cast your actors, sort out your equipment, and so on. In a commercial production, you also agree the budget, arrange financing, and sort out all the legal issues at this stage. Any film producer will tell you that time spent in preproduction is never wasted. Effort spent in preproduction will save you five times that amount of effort in production, and 20 times that effort in postproduction. 'Spend lots of time in preproduction – it will save loads of time and especially frustration later down the road,' urges Jason Choi. 'People in the film business say this stuff a lot, but they don't say it just because it sounds cool. It's absolutely true.'

PRODUCTION

You create what you're going to work with. In the case of machinima, you make models, create custom animations, record your dialogue, and shoot your footage. This is often the shortest part of the process. If you've done your preproduction properly, it should run like clockwork; every time you find yourself wishing you'd sorted something out beforehand, that's an indication that something went wrong in preproduction.

POSTPRODUCTION

You finish everything off. The line between production and post is often blurred, especially in the case of scripted machinima where editing and filming are inextricably linked. Post includes editing, dubbing, adding sound and music, special effects, and preparing the film for release. Many film directors argue that post is where the film is actually created. You can completely change the look and feel of a film in post, as numerous 'Director's Cut' versions attest. It's also your last chance to fix anything that didn't go quite right. Be prepared to spend a long time on postproduction.

Even if you're only doing a short film, and you're working on your own, you should learn to follow the production process almost religiously. You'll be glad you did.

Unreal Confrontation (2004),
by Jens Schöbel, shows what can
*be done with assets from **Unreal***
***Tournament 2004**.*

KNOWING YOUR LIMITATIONS

Making machinima is fun but hard work, and it's easy to get discouraged and give up. Many of the best machinima take months to complete. Most machinima projects are simply abandoned when the creators realize they've bitten off more than they can chew. 'I have a lot of respect for a machinima maker who has simply completed a piece,' says veteran machinimator Ken Thain. 'That is a major achievement in itself. As it stands today, it takes a unique person of artistic vision and technological mastery to create a machinima piece. Those who have done it show they have the drive to achieve their vision. Then it's just a matter of refining their skills and raising the bar.'

The key to a successful project is knowing your limitations and working within them. There are three main areas you need to consider: time, skill, and resources.

Running out of time is the usual reason why most media projects fail. Machinima has to fit in around family, work, school, and other commitments. A grandiose epic is a wonderful aspiration, but it's not necessarily the best place to start.

When it comes to skill, work within what you can do. If you can't model, then use in-game assets. If you don't want to do voices, or you can't write dialogue, do a silent piece or a music video.

Resources include people, equipment, and money. While money isn't often a factor for amateur productions, it can be significant. Tools such as FRAPS cost a few pounds – it's not much, but it all adds up. More important are resources such as sound recording equipment, hard disk space, and your cast and crew. If you only have two puppeteers, you're going to be limited in what you can do. You can often scrounge resources, but unless they're as dedicated as you are, their generosity can rapidly wear thin.

Thain offers this advice: 'Start small and simply complete the process, from conception to release. Write up a simple script, scribble out some images of the story through the camera's eye, grab some maps, character models, etc. and put together a story. Add your name and release. It does not have to be a masterpiece but you will quickly come to terms with the real deal of making machinima. You can then take the experience of your first production, examine the strengths and weaknesses of both yourself and the technology, and set the bar on the next production. With each piece you will grow in talent, skill, and knowledge, not only of the technology and machinima-making process but also your potential as a film-maker.'

'Begin practising your craft, and don't be afraid to make a few mistakes along the way. During college, I worked with Bryan Singer (director of *The Usual Suspects* and *The X-Men* films) on a student film – one that I'm sure he would sooner forget. Needless to say, he had to make that film before he made some of his future great ones,' says Paul Marino.

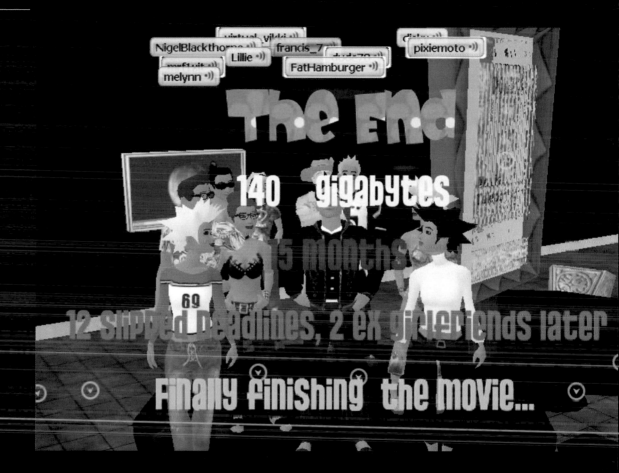

*The true cost of making machinima... **The AVIE Who Shagged Me** (2004), by Munly 'FatHamburger' Leong*

*LEFT: Ubisoft's **XIII** (2003) has a uniquely 'comic strip' look to it, which would be a challenge for any machinimator.*
*BELOW LEFT: **Testimony of a Paraqeet** (2004) blends comic book speech balloons with **Unreal Tournament** to create a unique look while sidestepping the issue of dialogue recording.*
*BELOW: **Nesmut** (2004), by Artemis Software, makes up for the lack of close-ups with body movement to show who is talking.*
*RIGHT: Blizzard's **World of Warcraft** (2004) offers great potential for machinima.*

As we showed you at the end of the previous section, choosing your machinima engine is probably the single most important decision you'll make. With the number of different game engines currently on the market, the choice is perhaps a little bewildering.

The easy solution is to use the engine from your favourite game as your machinima tool. In some ways, that's a perfectly fine solution. It's probably the engine you're most familiar with, so it'll be easiest for you to use. On the other hand, because it's a good game engine doesn't mean it's a good machinima engine, and your familiarity with it in a game context isn't necessarily relevant in a machinima context. Being able to devastate your enemies with a biorifle in *Unreal Tournament* has nothing to do with being able to manipulate 3D models and scripts in *UnrealEd*.

Your choice of engine will define exactly what you can and cannot do in your film. For a start, it determines what techniques you can use. Few games support full scripting, so you'll probably be forced to do some puppeteering. This decision will affect your approach right from the start, in that for puppeteering you'll need a cast, a server, and a way of capturing, storing, and editing footage. Multiplayer capability is essential for puppeteered machinima.

Consider camera angles. Can you get in close enough to your subjects? If the camera is always too high, the viewer can't relate well to the characters. A constant camera angle becomes dull. Can you use a sniperscope or binoculars view to get in close?

Consider levels of detail. Newer engines have much more detailed models than old ones, particularly in close-up. 'Avoid the use of old engines, and stick to newer ones. Think of it this way — would someone be more interested and would the film turn out for the better if it was done in a brand new engine like *Half-Life 2* or something ancient like *Quake*?' asks Xanatos.

On the other hand, that level of detail comes at a price. *Doom 3* character models and sets took hundreds of hours to produce. Unless you're using in-game assets, be prepared to spend just as much time creating your own. Anthony Bailey puts the case for older engines: 'Although the newest engines will make for the shiniest visuals, I would try to go with something established rather than experimenting with the sparkliest alleged next great thing. Rendering quality ages quickly. Storytelling quality does not, so choose something you can work well in.'

Find out how much of the engine you can tweak. Can you, for example, remove the HUD? What aspects of the game can you mod? Does the game provide enough for you to do something interesting with it? Do you have the freedom of expression you need? 'I strongly advocate using something open enough that you can get in and change it in key places if and when you need to. The tools can be at least as important as the core engine', says Bailey.

Most importantly, though, become very familiar with your engine. It's your studio set, your wardrobe department, your camera, and your lighting rig all in one.

'**Don't be discouraged by the learning curve and always try something different. Give different engines a chance and be creative with your ideas. They all have their strengths and weaknesses and so really there is no easiest.'**

ATUSSA SIMON, *Machinimator*

CREATIVE SOLUTIONS TO TECHNICAL PROBLEMS

- Take this to Schumann. Today.

- Now? You're joking!

© Mforma Europe Ltd.

© Mforma Europe Ltd.

The range of film genres and styles has largely been shaped not by opportunities but by limitations. The whole of film noir, for example, evolved as a response to tight shooting schedules and limited sets, which could have proved a handicap but which the film-makers turned instead into a stylistic statement.

The responses that you make to limitations will comprise part of your individual idiom of expression. Faced with any limitation, your goal as a film-maker is not only to find a work-around solution, but to turn that limitation to your advantage.

As they say in software development when coming up with a desperate explanation for something unexpected or avoidable: 'It's a feature.'

Consider a scene in which a character has to open a letter. Without some custom animation, that's going to be tricky. But there are many ways to get around this.

The easiest solution is to point the camera somewhere else while he's opening the letter – his face is a good option. You could call this the conjurer's solution, as it is similar to a conjurer's sleight-of-hand. We don't notice the cut away from his hands because the shot makes narrative sense. The contents of the envelope are a mystery and, as the viewers, we want in on that mystery, and the shot teases us. It makes us want to peek out of the frame, and while we're metaphorically

hopping about for a better view, we're distracted from the real reason the film-maker cut to that view.

But there are other ways we could have got round the problem. Most obvious is the cheat solution – cutting in a close-up of non-machinima footage showing a real actor's hands. Gerry Anderson and his team often used this solution on the *Thunderbirds* puppet TV series.

Alternatively, you might try the clown's solution. For instance, the character could pause, look right at the camera, then deliberately turn away from us while opening the envelope. This makes a virtue of necessity, aiming for comic effect by overtly drawing attention to the need to conceal the hands. Another version of the same solution is to have the character turn around and open the letter with his back to the viewer, secretively, creating extra mystery. The movement of his hands and head suggests what's going on, forcing viewers to use their imagination and engage more closely with the story.

The ideal solution is the film-maker's solution, which is to tell your story in a way that doesn't keep bumping up against obstacles like this. Cinema is an economical medium. Instead of showing the character opening a letter, you can come later into the scene to show the torn envelope and the look on his face as he reads the letter.

SARAH: I saw her in my dream.   EDWARD: Such creatures are not to be trusted.

ABOVE LEFT: For their Cold War thriller **Berlin Assassins** *(1999), nGame achieved close-ups by matting in painted characters with better facial detail. Subtitles were used instead of sound.*
ABOVE, TOP: **Consanguinity** *(2004), by Damien Valentine, also uses subtitles instead of speech.*

ABOVE: In **Halo,** *you can't see anyone's mouth. The convention in* **Red vs Blue** *(2003), as in anime, is that whoever is speaking shuffles around to attract your attention.*

START WITH THE STORY

'Remember, it's all about the story – regardless of the medium.'

PAUL MARINO, *Animator and machinimator*

Storywriting needs to be approached on at least three levels at once. When you ask yourself what your film is about, you need to be able to give at least three different answers.

The easiest one to understand is the plot. It is often argued by anthropologists, literary theorists, and mythologists that there are only a limited number of possible plots. Everything you can think of is only a variation on one or more of those basic plots, so don't worry if yours doesn't seem particularly original at first. If you want to make life really easy on yourself, pick a story you know well, and adapt it. *The Magnificent Seven*, one of the great Westerns, is simply an adaptation of Kurosawa's samurai epic, *Seven Samurai*. Kurosawa himself wasn't averse to

Throughout this book, we've quoted machinimators from all backgrounds talking about story. This isn't just writers trying to promote writing above other aspects of film-making. The story is the reason people will watch – or switch off – your film.

Choosing an engine and choosing a story go hand-in-hand. You need to ensure your engine is capable of telling your story. In some cases, your engine will constrain the types of story you can tell. If you're filming in *Battlefield 1942*, you're pretty well limited to war stories in one form or another. However, there are war stories, and there are war stories. Gut-wrenchers like *Saving Private Ryan* and propaganda pieces like *Ill Met by Moonlight* couldn't be more different.

transplanting Shakespeare to feudal Japan – *Ran* and *Throne of Blood* are based on *King Lear* and *Macbeth*.

Where you can start to bring in some originality is in the characterization. The audience has to care about who these people are. To a large extent, the people are more important than the plot; this film is about them, not what they do. In short pieces, you have a limited time to get the characters across, which is hard. Their speech, their body style, and their dress need to convey their personality as much as their actions. In a longer piece, character development is important. The audience needs to see the characters changed by their experiences, perhaps sadder and wiser, or perhaps just less shallow.

The third level is much more abstract and requires you to step right back from the story. Every story, particularly drama, needs a theme. You don't need to go in for any heavy-handed moralizing, but you should think about what your story is saying to people. The themes can be simple: betrayal, revenge, or heroism – or more complex: facing up to fear, the price of friendship, or choosing between loyalty and honour. Theme is also affected by mood, and this involves another raft of important decisions. Is the film lighthearted or serious? Action-packed or languid?

Once you know what your story is about, you're ready to start turning it into a film.

*ABOVE: Ken Thain's **The Everseason** (2004) and Digital Yolk's **Bot** (2004, LEFT) both feature strong characters and interesting storylines that get the viewer hooked instantly.*

STORYBOARDING

Before you start filming, you should know exactly what your film is going to look like. You should be so familiar with it that you can watch it in your head, from beginning to end. Once you can do this, you can think like a film director.

Being able to visualize an entire film is a very rare skill. You may have some particular sequences or shots in mind, but the chances are there will be gaps. The favoured solution to this is the storyboard. Part planning tool, part aide-mémoire, it allows you to plan out every single shot in the film.

A typical storyboard looks like a comic. It consists of a simple drawing of each shot. The drawing quality doesn't have to be good; it only has to be enough for you to tell what's in the shot. It's usual to add on arrows to show movement of characters or cameras. What you need to focus on is who is in the shot, and in particular the framing. If Geoff and Cynthia are having an argument, where are you going to place the cameras? How many cameras do you need? Will they be by the window or by the door?

Deciding how your scene is going to look before you film it has several advantages. For a start, it should mean that everything runs smoothly on the day. The actors and cameramen will know what they've got to do. You know what shots you're after, and when you've got them, you can move on.

Equally importantly, you know what you need to build to get the shot, and what special effects you need. If a particular area is only going to be seen from one angle, you don't need to worry about creating the rest of the set.

Location scouting is an important feature of storyboarding for machinima. If you're using sets from games, you need to revisit the game levels with your director's eye on. You only need to be able to use small segments of a level to imply a much bigger place. In *Robin Hood: Prince of Thieves*, Kevin Costner and Mary Elizabeth Mastrantonio have a scene outside the door to a castle. The scene was shot at Old Wardour Castle in Wiltshire, England, most of which is in ruins. However, with careful camera placement, the ruins are out of shot, and the castle seems complete. The machinimator needs to develop a similar sense of lateral thinking, finding interesting locations and incorporating them into the storyboard.

Once the storyboarding is complete, you should be able to produce a shot list. This tells you exactly what shots you need, what locations, cast, and props are needed for each shot, and assigns a number to each shot. Computer-based storyboarding tools, although they are not to everyone's taste, can automate production of shot lists.

*LEFT: **Storyboard Tools**, an easy-to-use free tool, developed by Ian Pegler.*
*RIGHT BELOW: The storyboard for Short Fuze's **No Licence** (2004) was crude, but adequate for creating a complete shot list detailing what was required for each scene.*
*RIGHT ABOVE: Ken Thain assembled the hand-drawn storyboard of **Rebel vs Thug** (2003) into a test version of the completed film.*

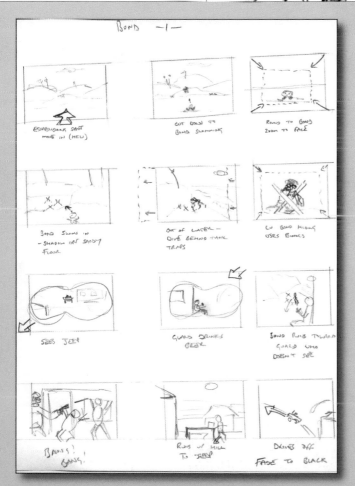

BOND —1—

ESTABLISHING SHOT MOVE IN (HELI)	CUT DOWN TO BOND SLAMMING	RUNS TO BOND ZOOM TO FACE
BOND SLAMS IN - SHADOW ON SANDY FLOOR	OUT OF LATER - DIVE BEHIND TANK TRAPS	CU BOND HIDING USES BINOCS
SEES JEEP	GUARD DRINKS BEER	BOND RUNS TOWARD GUARD WHO DOESN'T SEE
BANGS! BANG!	RUNS UP HILL TO JEEP	DRIVES OFF FADE TO BLACK

Scene 3

Description

BOND is making his getaway and charges through the GUARD POST leading to the AIRFIELD. He is chased by various MINIONS in different vehicles, but manages to make them crash.

This scene requires stunt driving: BOND is in-car throughout the scene. This will require some improvisation depending on how many machinimators we can get on the day — we may only use 2 chase cars instead of 4, for example.

Location

Central Camp & nearby trackway

Characters

BOND
MINIONS

Vehicles

JEEP
JEEP WITH TOW or MG
DUNE BUGGY x 2

Props

Minion: Rocket Launcher (TOW)

Scene 3, Shot 1

Description

JEEP RUNS THRU GUARD SLAPPED

Shot of the GUARD POST. MINIONS are standing bored. VEHICLES are parked either side. BOND drives into shot from L and charges straight through the gateway without pausing. MINIONS don't react until it's too late. Hold for next shot.

Cast

BOND
MINIONS (Lots)

Notes

PLANNING VS IMPROVISATION

Now that we've impressed upon you the absolute necessity of having a storyboard and planning everything in advance, it's time to remind you that one of the great strengths of machinima is that you don't need to do that all the time.

When you actually arrive on set, it always looks subtly different to the way that you imagined it. It doesn't matter how many times you've played the level, and how well you've run through the scene in your head, you can always see another way when it comes to the crunch. Those serendipitous moments will produce your most inspired pieces of film-making.

On a film set, time is money. When you've got dozens or even hundreds of actors, crew, caterers, and drivers all hanging around being paid on a daily rate (with hefty union-mandated overtime payments if you keep them beyond their agreed hours), you're racking up a phenomenal cost every hour you're on set. You need to keep the shooting time down to an absolute minimum. If you decide that you don't like the way a particular scene is turning out and want to do it differently, that's an expensive decision. Worse than that, it could land you with all sorts of insuperable logistical problems: you may

only have hired the location for a few days, or your stars could be booked on another production. As a result, production has to go smoothly. An indecisive director is a producer's worst nightmare. Getting something in the bag that works is far more important than wasting money searching for that elusive perfect shot. Hence everything is planned down to the last detail in preproduction. Rewriting a scene and messing with the storyboard may take a few days, but that's nothing compared to the cost of an extra day on set with a full crew.

Until machinima hits the big time, amateur machinimators are unlikely to have to face this problem. Throwing away a large chunk of work may be irksome, but it's hardly likely to foreshadow financial doom. If you're working on your own, as is the case with most scripted machinima, you can feel free to mess about as much as you like, trying different ways of shooting the scene, until you're completely happy with it.

Even if you've got a few friends acting as puppeteers, they usually won't mind trying the same scene several times. After all, they're doing this because it's fun. You may well find that they want to have some input into the scene. This could be minor changes, such as suggesting different movements or different camera angles, or they could suggest moving the whole scene to a different location, or changing things even more radically. You don't need to adopt the strict hierarchy that goes with a commercial production; take ideas from anyone and everyone. It doesn't matter if they don't work – filming is cheap, and you can throw away the bad takes with a single keystroke.

*ABOVE LEFT AND RIGHT: The slightly unpredictable nature of the AI in **The Movies** (2005) means that some improvisation is inevitable. RIGHT: When filming a stunt film like **Battlefield Stuntacular** (2004), some planning is always required, but sometimes the best thing is to let the crew go crazy and see what they can do!*

'The Golden Rule is that there are no golden rules.'
GEORGE BERNARD SHAW

Zen'Sen: The Guardian (2004), by Sebastian Tuschy, is a machinima film promoting **Zen'Sen: A Tournament of the Fallen**, a mod for **Unreal Tournament**. Both film and game are heavily influenced by anime. The film makes extensive use of postprocessing to create stylish imagery.

Whether you're going down the route of working exactly to a script, or you're relying on spontaneity to generate your film, preparation and planning is essential to running an effective shoot and a happy set.

Unless you're going for total improvisation, you need some idea of what you're trying to achieve in a session, both in terms of the number of scenes you plan to shoot, and what's going to be in each scene. If you've storyboarded the scenes, you should have a shot list prepared, which will tell you exactly what you will be doing in terms of camera placement, actor movement, props required, and so on. If you are really organized, you should plan a shooting sequence in advance. You don't need to film shots in the order they will appear in the finished product. It is often much more efficient to set up specific camera angles on a set, and then film everything you will need from that camera angle. This can be a little disorienting for the actors, but you need to make sure they understand what they are doing.

For example, Mike and Jeff have a conversation outside a bar, then go inside and start a fight with Ryan. The barman throws all three of them out, and they continue arguing in the street. You can shoot the street scenes before and after the fight back to back, then film the bar brawl later. Just remember that if any of them picks up bruises or torn clothes in the fight, you'll need to put this in between the two sequences.

Filming machinima generates a vast quantity of video files, particularly if you're planning on a fast-cutting sequence. Finding the shot you're after can be a nightmare. It's essential to make sure that you store all of your files in a way that's easy to work with. FRAPS typically assigns filenames that are a combination of the game name and the date, such as *BF1942 2004-07-16 08-10-33-96.avi*. That's great in that it's unique, but hardly the most friendly way to find a file in a hurry. It's much easier to rename the file to something more accessible, such as *NoLic-Sc02-04-03-MK.avi*. That tells the editor immediately that the file is from the film *No Licence*, Scene 2, Shot 4, Take 3, shot from the camera controlled by Matt Kelland. When looking at the storyboard for a particular shot, he can immediately find all the files with all the different takes, and choose the one he wants.

For maximum efficiency, you should write down a text description of each shot you take. For example, we might note that *NoLic-Sc02-04-03-MK.avi* shows 'Henchman being shot, falls down steps', while *NoLic-Sc02-04-04-MK.avi* shows 'Henchman being shot, falls back into room', and *NoLic-Sc02-04-05-MK.avi* is 'Henchman being shot, not a good take'. Your editor will really appreciate the extra bit of work you put in on the day!

And finally, put all the footage into a single place. If you're filming with several cameras, you could end up with video files scattered around many different computers.

CASE STUDY: PAPPY BOYINGTON

Ian Kristensen, better known among the machinima community as Pappy Boyington, is a native of British Columbia, Canada. He specializes in making action films in *Battlefield 1942*, often with a fairly large cast. He talks about working with so many people.

Working with a large crew has proven to be challenging to say the least. Even people you would have considered to be a great help cannot resist shooting their buddy at the most inopportune moments. Most of my crew is over 30 years old, and I'm 38, and still we run into this problem trying to set scenes up to shoot. Of course, we are doing this for fun and not profit, so I like to allow a little room for the guys to 'goof off'.

What I've been doing for my latest film, *The River*, is offering a part in the film to whoever will show at 6pm on weekdays for an hour or two of shooting. We've had basically the same crew of ten or twelve guys turn up every day. Since we've had a few weeks to gel as a unit, things have really improved, and the guys realize when they can and can't goof around.

My advice to anyone wanting to direct a larger crew, or even a small crew, is pick people who can be patient while you set things up. Give them an area of the map to burn off excess energy that won't interfere with what you're setting up if they're not needed in the scene. You should try to include everyone in every scene, even if they're just extras walking from one building to the next. It will cut down on boredom if nothing else and give them a sense of worth.

Once you're ready, call a 'Cease Fire' and make sure that they all understand this means no shooting of anything by anyone or it could cost the whole crew more wasted time to reset the scene. Make sure everyone knows their parts and make sure they're ready before you call 'Action!'

In most cases you'll have to shoot the same scene several times to get the perfect shot, and also shoot it from different angles, but it gets easier every time you set it up. Record your rehearsals – they may be just the perfect look you were after!

You can always delete the files later. As soon as you have the basic scene planned out and people in place, let the cameras roll and don't miss out on anything. Once everything is set up, it's very easy to tell the team to set it up again. You can also let them know if anything needed tweaking from the take before, or if it all went perfectly and please do it the same way again. This is way easier than seeing the film later and not being happy with it, then trying to set the whole scene up again and get people in their places.

It can be intimidating at first, but once everyone knows your voice on Teamspeak they will pipe down while you are directing. As the action unfolds, try to comment all the way through, such as giving locations of oncoming attackers and cueing people to ready for their part in the scene. Give as much direction as you can before the scene, and if at all possible, let the actors time scenes themselves and in essence cue themselves to respond. It's hard to cue every single person at the exact right moment, so if you can tell them, for example, 'When actor "A" gets to this point, actor "B" will perform this action' it will make the scene unfold much smoother. Things can happen very quickly and it's too easy to miss a cue for someone to start their actions.

Practise, practise, practise, and last but not least, thank the cast for their participation!

One last little tip. It helps to knock the health down of anyone you want to be killed in a certain scene. We have a ritual now called 'five in the foot'. Five pistol shots in the foot will get your health down to where one bullet from anyone will send you to your grave. The guys love that part. The hard part is getting 'only' five in the foot. Everyone's so eager to help you nearly die!

RIGHT TOP: ***A Hard Road*** *(2004)*
CENTRE: ***The River*** *(2004)*
BOTTOM: ***Dead Cities*** *(2004)*

LOOKING LIKE A FILM

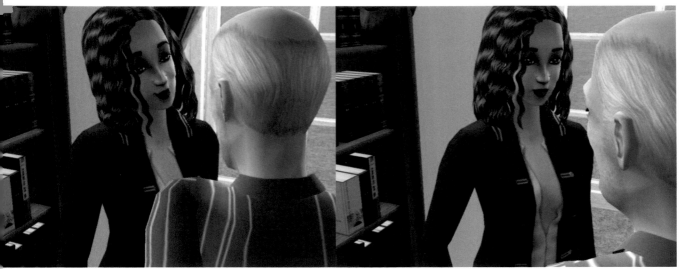

Audiences aren't supposed to realize it, but watching a film is as much about how the they interpret the film as what the film-maker puts on the screen. As viewers, we have learned from an early age how to make sense of a film, and how to draw inferences from what we see. Film has a grammar, just like writing, and you need to know how to use that grammar to express yourself.

This is the art of cinematography. It's the craft that professional directors spend years learning, and what distinguishes a good production from the mediocre. It's also what distinguishes a film made in a game engine from clips of gameplay edited together. It's clearly impossible to compress a complete film course into a few paragraphs, but here are a few key rules you ignore at your peril.

The most basic rule of cinematography is called 'crossing the line'. To put it simply, you should always stay on one side or the other of the action, or the viewer will get confused. Imagine two characters in a conversation. Now visualize a line drawn between them. When you cross the line, the characters will appear to switch sides on-screen.

Following on from this rule is the concept of continuity. This isn't about spotting those embarrassing mistakes like glasses of water that magically refill themselves mid-scene. This is about implying to the viewer that what they see in one scene or shot continues into another. If you see a shot of the Eiffel Tower,

then the film cuts to an office interior, you will assume that the office is in Paris. Continuity also extends to the details of shots. If a character leaves a scene in one direction and immediately appears in the next scene, you normally expect him to enter from the same direction. Incidentally, one convention of films, perhaps based on the way we read, is that travelling from left to right normally implies going somewhere, while travelling right to left implies returning.

The way a camera moves in a film has meaning. Moving a camera in towards something invites viewers to focus their attention on that thing, and also asks them to remember that during the next shot. Close-ups bring the viewer into the characters and engage them emotionally rather than intellectually. Pulling the camera away asks the viewer to focus on the big picture rather than one specific thing, or else signifies the end of a segment. Following a moving person at a set distance asks the viewer to identify with that person; tracking them as they move past the camera and away asks them to identify instead with an observer.

And finally, there is composition. Treat every shot like a photograph, and think about where you want the viewer to look. Some shots are just there to look stunning – that's OK – but most have to advance the story in some way. You don't need to put the centre of attention in the centre of the screen – it's often more effective to draw their focus off to one side.

'Take the time to learn some standard film techniques and apply them to your film. The quality will show, and you will be glad you did.'

JASON CHOI, *Machinimator*

LEFT: The framing of these two shots is subtly different. In the first, the viewer is aware of two people in the frame. In the second, the back of the man's head, by being moved right up to the edge of the frame, effectively reduces the area of the screen, and the viewer focuses more on the woman.
RIGHT: Crossing the line: the man is now on the left of the picture. It's a nice shot, but you shouldn't use it in the same sequence as the previous ones.
BELOW: Interesting composition: the mirror allows the viewer to see both sides of the subjects – and the camera isn't reflected either! The heads in the three-shot are all at different heights and distances, creating an asymmetric shot.

LOSING THE GAME

'Game style is becoming more and more common in film-making. This is particularly true in action blockbuster type films like *Phantom Menace*, *Spiderman*, or *The Hulk*. I think it's because there is going to be a videogame tie-in for all these games, and they are targeted to a generation of young males who are very familiar with the videogame style (grammar) of storytelling.'

INGRID MOON, *Film-maker and machinimator*

RIGHT: *By adding film tone and scratches to the video image, Ian Kristensen creates the look of an old newsreel in* **A Hard Road** *(2004).* **Halo** *films such as* **Out for Blood** *(2003, FAR RIGHT) tend to be in extreme widescreen to remove the HUD.* BELOW: *A typical gamer's HUD, from* **Battlefield 1942: Desert Combat**. *All that extra information needs to be removed or hidden.*

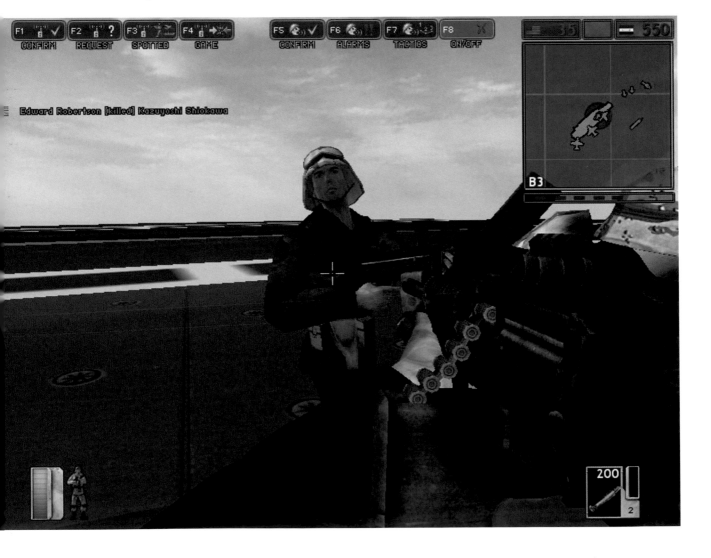

Edward Robertson [killed] Kazuyoshi Shiokawa

Most machinima shouldn't look like a game. The first thing you'll have to do is remove anything onscreen that's designed as a gameplay aid, such as health meters, ammunition, weapons, and so on. This needs to be done before filming, or you'll end up recording the game data as well as the footage. Many games allow you to do this with a special command. In *Battlefield 1942*, you simply type ~ while playing the game to bring up the command console, then type in HUD 0. Other games require an entry in a config file, or starting the game with specific options.

You can enhance the film-like quality of your machinima in many other ways. There are many plugins available that can mimic the different types of film stock; these change the colour balance of the film and sometimes even add in motion blur. Using these – or doing it by hand if you know how – removes a lot of the telltale gamelike clarity of the footage and helps reduce the feeling that you are watching a game. You can use any number of special effects in postproduction to do things that the game engine doesn't do; for example, in

If you can't get rid of the HUD that way, you can often block much of it out if you go to widescreen. Most games run in 4:3 aspect ratio. Films are typically much wider than that, ranging from 16:9 which is standard on modern TV programs to the ultra-widescreen 2.35:1 favoured by top-end Hollywood productions. Making your film widescreen will immediately give it a much more filmic look.

The easiest way to create a widescreen effect is to make a mask consisting of black strips at the top and bottom, leaving a transparent area of the appropriate shape in the middle of the screen. You then lay this over the top of your machinima in your video editing software. Of course, this will affect your composition, as you won't be able to see everything that you had before. You can shift the image vertically to choose the best part of the picture, but you have no horizontal freedom. A neat trick is to put thin strips of black tape on your monitor while filming so that you can see what the end result will look like with the mask on.

No Licence, video editor Phil South added in a focusing effect to a binocular shot, replicating what a camera would see, rather than what a game engine renders.

The finishing touches are the opening and closing sequences – titles and credits. The opening titles set the tone for the entire piece. It's worth spending effort on them, even if they're only a few seconds long. There are two schools of thought with respect to credits. In film, the fashion is for extensive credits, listing everyone who took part, in every capacity. Since the only payment most of the crew is going to get in a machinima is in the form of a credit, this is perfectly justified. However, in a short machinima piece, this is often impractical, because the credits begin to outweigh the film, and the same names keep cropping up over and over again as writer, director, producer, voice actor, editor, model-maker, and so on. This soon starts to look like vanity. A good compromise solution is to credit a film as 'created by' the key personnel and then list everyone else under the heading 'with' or 'with thanks to'.

ADDING SOUND

Sound always gets mentioned last in books about film. It's often an afterthought when games are made. Film-makers and game developers alike are seduced by the visual allure of their creations. This is a dangerous trap to fall into. Sound is at least as important as the onscreen imagery, and deserves at least as much of your attention.

The easy option for machinimators is to use the sounds that come with the game, and just take the sounds from the original recording. This has the added advantage that the sounds are usually ready-mixed to match the camera position, both in terms of volume and stereo positioning.

Where you need to be a little clever with using sounds this way is when you cut between shots. While it may be accurate for sound levels to change suddenly when you change viewpoints, it doesn't always make for a good soundtrack. You therefore need to cut the soundtrack and the video track slightly out of sync to ensure a smooth transition. You also need to be careful when you edit in order to preserve continuity between different shots. Say you have a sequence with a car screeching around a corner and crashing into a wall. The initial footage will record the complete tyre squeal, engine noise, and crash. If you edit that to show the initial skid, cut away to a horrified bystander,

and then back to the impact, the sequence may well end up a second or so shorter. The scene will probably be more exciting as a result, but your original sound sequence will no longer fit. Your options are to rebuild the sound sequence and trim it down, or to create one afresh.

Creating original sounds is time-consuming but highly rewarding. The easiest solution is to use a sound-effects library. You can buy sounds on CD or individually online. These can give you everything from footsteps, gunfire, and vehicle engines to birdsong, factory noises, and whirring computer disks.

Building up the sounds is always more complicated than you expect it to be. Every time you watch the film, you will see something else that should have a sound. Eventually you will start putting in sounds for things you can't see. In one sequence in Short Fuze's *No Licence*, the hero shoots a guard in a beach hut. The sounds at that point include the gunshot and the cartridge ejecting, the sound of the dead guard falling, a slight scuff of feet as the hero adjusts his position, waves on the beach, a faint wind noise, and a flock of startled birds flying into the sky. All you can see onscreen is the hero pointing the gun into the hut – the guard, the beach, and the birds are all offscreen and suggested by the soundtrack.

OPPOSITE: *Good-quality dialogue is essential for most forms of comedy: the entire premise of Binary Studios'* **Bouncer Please** *(2004) is the repartee between the bouncer and the people who are trying to get in.*

BELOW: *Short Fuze's* **No Licence** *(2004) soundtrack consists of up to 15 sounds simultaneously, including dialogue, vehicle noises, weapons, and ambience.*

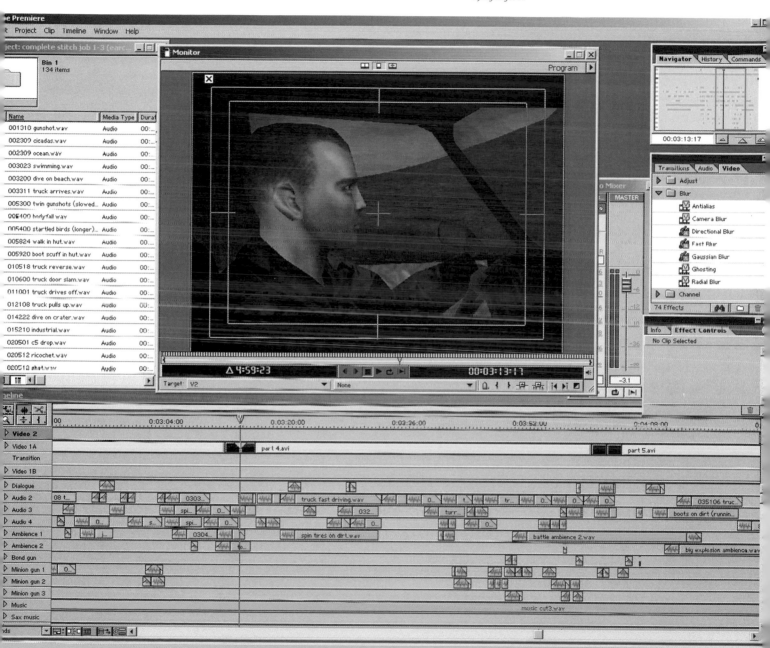

ADDING SOUND 2

DIALOGUE

There are two schools of thought when it comes to dialogue: recording before, and recording after. Some groups, such as the *Red vs Blue* team, like to record the dialogue in advance and act to the dialogue. This means that they can make sure that their actions match the voices exactly. If you are using lip synch tools such as *Impersonator*, you need to record dialogue in advance, since the models' facial movements are directly controlled by the speech track.

Other machinimators prefer to record the dialogue afterwards. This approach allows them more freedom of improvisation on set. If necessary, the script can be rewritten to take account of the revised action and editing.

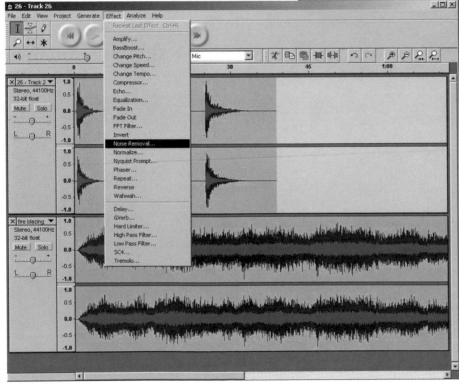

Music and sound tools:
LEFT: **Audacity**, a freeware sound editing program, compared to **Cakewalk Sonar** (ABOVE), the professional equivalent.
FAR RIGHT: **Jammer** allows you to compose music without being able to play an instrument.
ABOVE RIGHT: **Cool Edit Pro** is another popular sound editor.

BALANCING

The trickiest bit of all when it comes to sound is balancing. You have to be able to hear music, dialogue, and sound effects, all at the same time, and you also have to direct your listener's ear to the most important element. During a furious gun battle, at one moment, perhaps the speech needs to dominate, then the sound of a rumbling tank track has to attract their attention.

If you listen closely to a film, you will notice that the soundtrack rarely matches the visuals precisely. There is much less dynamic range in a film than you might expect. Things that should be loud are often quiet, and faint sounds are often unduly emphasized. Whispers are frequently as loud as normal conversations, and full-on yells are surprisingly muted. If you see a rebel soldier on a hill shouting defiance, and the director cuts from a long shot to a close-up, the sound rarely changes in volume to match.

Start by identifying the key elements at each point that you want your viewer to listen to, and then bring in the rest of the sounds to an appropriate level. In particular, remember that music doesn't have to stay at a constant level throughout.

DISTRIBUTION

Now that you've made your masterpiece, you'll want to show it off to all and sundry. The easiest solution is to post it on the Net on a site like www.machinima.com. Your key consideration now has to be bandwidth. Even in these days of increasingly widespread broadband, the Net does not have unlimited capacity for distributing huge files, and there are limits on how long viewers are prepared to wait before they can watch your film.

Uncompressed video is so huge that it is completely impractical – even DVDs are compressed. You therefore need to compress your film down to a manageable size.

All video codecs degrade the video quality to some degree; the skill comes in knowing how to get the best from different codecs in order to get the best compression for the best quality. If you use the popular DivX codec, it works best when used in multipass encoding mode. On the initial pass, the DivX software first analyses the video and calculates how best to compress it. On subsequent passes, it refines its compression algorithm, and gradually reduces the file size while retaining quality. This can be quite time-consuming, but the results are well worth the time spent.

Simply using a codec to compress your video isn't enough. The viewers need to be able to decode it at the other end, which means they need a copy of the same codec. Make sure that you provide a link to a site where the viewers can download the codec, particularly if you're using an unusual one – and don't expect them to pay for a codec!

You can get a huge reduction in file size by reducing the size of the image. A 1024 x 768 frame contains 786,432 pixels. Reducing that to 640 x 480 cuts that down to 307,200, less than half the original data. Going all the way down to 320 x 240 slices each frame to just 76,800 pixels, not even a tenth of the original. It is quite common to release films in two versions, a low-resolution version with a small image and high compression, and a high-resolution version with a larger screen and less compression.

If you release your film as a demo rather than a video, you don't have to worry about most of these issues. Instead, you need to ensure that the demo will install easily, and that viewers know what they have to do to watch the film. It's not reasonable to expect most people to spend hours messing around with individual files, and you must allow for the possibility that their computer is setup differently from yours.

If you plan to release your film on DVD, remember that many countries have systems where all films must be submitted to a ratings body before they can be distributed. Also be aware that even if there is no such body in your country, there may still be restrictions for people purchasing your film over the Internet.

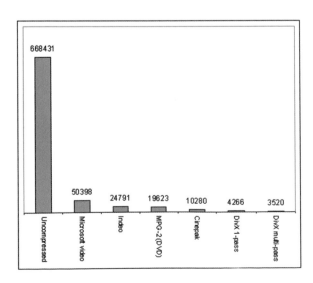

LEFT: Compressing a one-minute long 800 x 600 video has dramatic effects (size in bytes)

*ABOVE TOP: Compare the quality of **Red vs Blue** formatted for DVD and Web download; note the fuzzy edges on the armour and blurred background.*

BELOW: **TMPGEnc3.0** by Pegasys, one of the most useful video encoding tools, supports a variety of codecs. The DivX codec allows you to choose between quality and performance, and to optimize for different viewing setups.

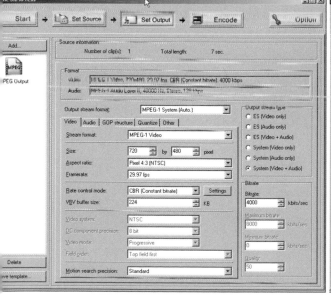

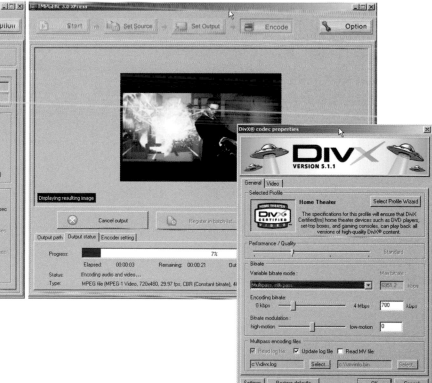

CASE STUDY: *NO LICENCE*

Short Fuze's *No Licence* was created in summer 2004 as a short test piece using *Battlefield 1942*. Acclaimed by the machinima community, it is an homage to the opening sequence of a James Bond film, a mini-movie in five minutes that has nothing to do with the main story but sets the audience up for the ride to come. Creators Matt Kelland and Dave Lloyd take you behind the scenes.

The main criteria were that the film had to be quick and easy to create on a minimal budget, and it had to demonstrate that we could generate exciting content that didn't look like footage of someone playing a game. We decided to use *BF 1942*, because it contains plenty of good possibilities for action, and was designed for multiplayer use. It has a good range of animations, including swimming and diving for cover, and has some basic body postures, such as looking around, and eye movement. In addition, it lends itself to easy modification, and there are a number of free mod tools available for it that are supported by the developers.

We decided to use the *Desert Combat* mod, which brings in modern tanks, aircraft, weapons, and uniforms. We then discovered a map of Easter Island, and realized that it offered great possibilities for a Bond-like action sequence. The volcano immediately suggested Blofeld's lair in *You Only Live Twice*. We played around on the map for a few hours and came up with a number of locations for good action sequences, such as a car chase, a MiG taking off through explosions, and a fight in the airbase.

The storyboard was written up in a couple of hours – literally on the back of an envelope – and was then turned into a shot list and asset list that detailed everything needed for the shoot.

We made a few mods to the game using *3D Studio Max*, *BattleCraft*, and the *Battlefield Mod Development Toolkit*: these included the uniforms, the rocket, and the hidden base. We converted the Easter Island map from its original *BF 1942* format to the *Desert Combat* format, and updated some of the buildings from Pacific beach huts to modern factory units. Mods took around four days.

Shooting took place over a two-day period and took about 14 hours including setup and takedown. We used a crew of between one and four people, working in a single room. For most of the shots, we only needed two people, and we only had the full crew for the major action sequences. As a result, *No Licence* was largely shot out of sequence. By the time we finished, we had over 40GB of footage.

Postproduction was done remotely, with the team working from home in different parts of the country and sending files

via the Internet. We used Premiere to edit the footage into the finished sequence and add special effects such as camera blur for the binocular focusing. We decided not to use in-game sounds, but to create sound effects from scratch. We produced a rough sound mix with a sound-effects library and cheap microphones, then sent that to Earcom, a professional sound production house, for a full-quality stereo music, foley, and dialogue mix. Postproduction took several weeks, as we went through several different cuts of the film, trimming it from seven minutes to under five.

The completed film was then rendered down from the uncompressed 10GB file into two smaller formats: a 50MB medium-quality DivX AVI for broadband download and a 300MB high-quality MPEG2 for DVD playback.

*Short Fuze's **No Licence** required numerous small modifications to be made to the basic **Battlefield 1942 Desert Combat** engine. The standard 'binocular view' was replaced with a custom binocular mask for a more filmic look, the soldiers were modified to give them bright orange uniforms and to make them easier to kill, and the 'explodamatic' allowed the special effects team to generate spectacular explosions.*

FURTHER READING AND WEB RESOURCES

More information on the skills required to become a machinimator is available from the following resources.

BOOKS

MACHINIMA

• **The Art of Machinima**, Paul Marino, Paraglyph Press, 2004

GENERAL

• **Rebel without a Crew**, Robert Rodriguez, Faber & Faber, 1996
• **The Complete Book of Scriptwriting**, J.Michael Straczynski, Titan Books, 1997
• **Story Structure**, Robert McKee, Methuen, 1999
• **The End of Celluloid: Film Futures in the Digital Age**, Matt Hanson, Rotovision, 2004

FILM TECHNIQUES

• **Film Directing Cinematic Motion: A Workshop for Staging Scenes**, Steven D. Katz, Michael Wiese Productions, 1997
• **Setting Up Your Shots: Great Camera Moves Every Filmmaker Should Know**, Jeremy Vineyard, Michael Wiese Productions, 2000
• **Grammar of the Film Language**, Daniel Arijon, Silman James Press, 1991
• **Film Directing Shot by Shot: Visualizing from Concept to Screen**, Steve Katz, Michael Wiese Productions, 1991
• **From Word to Image: Storyboarding and the Filmmaking Process**, Marcie Begleiter, Michael Wiese Productions, 2000
• **The 5 C's of Cinematography**, Joseph V Mascelli, Silman James Press, 1998
• **Painting with Light**, John Alton, University of California Press, 1995
• **Sound Design: The Expressive Power of Music, Voice and Sound Effects in Cinema**, David Sonnenschein (Editor), Michael Wiese Productions, 2001
• **In the Blink of an Eye: A Perspective on Film Editing**, Walter Murch, SIlman James Press, 2001
• **New Cinematographers**, Alexander Ballinger, Laurence King Publishing, 2004
• **Make Your Own Hollywood Movie**, Ed Gaskell, Ilex, 2004
• **The Guerrilla Filmmaker's Handbook**, Jones & Jolliffe, Continuum International Publishing Group, 2000
• **Producing Animation**, Catherine Winder & Zahra Dowlatabadi, Focal Press, 2001

SOFTWARE

• **LightWave 3D 8: 1001 Tips and Tricks**, Wordware Publishing, 2004
• **Stop Staring: Facial Modeling and Animation Done Right**, Jason Osipa, Sybex International, 2003
• **Modeling a Character in 3DS Max**, Paul Steed, Wordware Publishing, 2001
• **Animating Real-Time Game Characters**, Paul Steed, Charles River Media, 2002
• **Building a Digital Human**, Ken Brilliant, Charles River Media, 2003
• **Texturing: Concepts and Techniques**, Dennis Summers, Charles River Media, 2004
• **The Dark Side of Game Texturing**, David Franson, Course Technology, 2004
• **Audio Anecdotes: Tools, Tips, and Techniques for Digital Audio**, Ken Greenebaum & Ronen Barzel (Editors), AK Peters, 2003
• **After Effects and Photoshop: Animation and Production Effects for DV and Film**, Jeff Foster, Sybex International, 2004
• **Creative Titling with Premiere Pro**, Ed Gaskell, Ilex, 2004
• **Creative Titling with Final Cut Pro**, Diannah Morgan, Ilex, 2004
• **3D Games, Vol I & II**, Alan Watt & Fabio Policarpo, Addison Wesley, 2000
• **Gaming Hacks**, SImon Carless, O'Reilly, 2004

WEBSITES

MACHINIMA FILMS AND NEWS

http://www.machinima.com—*the best resource for all machinima information*
http://www.machinima.org—*Academy of Machinima Arts & Sciences*
http://www.3dfilmmaker.com—*3D filmmaker: news & reviews*
http://www.machinimag.com—*Machinimag—more news & reviews*
http://www.archive.org/movies/collection.php?collection=machinima
      —Internet Archive: Machinima

MACHINIMA AND GAME MOD SOFTWARE

http://halo.bungie.org/misc/cvmovies—*Halo Movie Starter Guide*
http://sv3.3dbuzz.com/vbforum/unr_main.php—*3D Buzz Unreal Technology*
http://www.gamasutra.com   *GamaSutra, the game developer's website*
http://udn.epicgames.com/Main/WebHome—*Unreal Developer Network*
http://battlefield1942.filefront.com—*BF1942 files*
http://www.planetbattlefield.com—*more BF1942 files*
http://www.planetquake.com—*everything Quake-related*
http://www.pcgamemods.com—*PC Game mods to download, plus tutorials*
http://www.turbosquid.com—*downloadable 3D models*
http://www.freefilmsoftware.co.uk—*storyboarding tools*
http://www.fileplanet.com   *downloads of many types*

GLOSSARY

AI (Artificial Intelligence): Software within a game engine that controls the actions of any character or object not controlled by the player.

Animation blending: Seamless transitions between different animation cycles, either sequentially, as when a character runs then jumps, or simultaneously, for example combining running legs and torso with a character reloading a weapon.

Aspect ratio: The description of the shape of a film image in terms of its width and height. 4:3 is the conventional TV or monitor shape, 16:9 is widescreen TV, and 2.35:1 is extreme cinematic widescreen.

Assets: The components that make up a game, such as 3D models, textures, sounds, and animation cycles.

Avatar: An in-game representation of a person.

Bandwidth: The speed at which data can be transmitted.

Capture: To collect and store information digitally. Motion capture stores information about a physical performance for use in animation. Video capture stores the onscreen representation of a game as a video file.

Codec (Compressor/Decompressor): A system used to reduce the size of a video file and then play it back. Different codecs store video in different ways, so the viewer usually needs to use the same codec as the person who compressed the file in order to see it.

Cut-scene: A noninteractive segment of a game, normally used for storytelling sequences.

Demo: A machinima film that runs within a game engine, rather than as a normal video file.

Emote: A gesture used by an in-game character to convey emotion, such as blowing a kiss, or frowning.

Engine: The key piece of software that runs the game or a part of the game.

Foley: The part of the soundtrack that comprises incidental sounds such as footfalls, doors opening, or background noises.

HUD (Head Up Display): Game information overlaid onto the screen such as health, ammunition remaining, or maps.

IP: Intellectual property.

Lip synch: Synchronizing the lip movements of characters to the dialogue, so it looks as if they are actually speaking.

MMORPG: Massively Multiplayer Online Role-playing Game.

Mod (Modification): A change to the retail version of a game.

Non-linear editor: Video editing software that allows you to access any part of the footage at will.

Pawn: A character in a scripted machinima.

Puppeteering: Creating on-screen action by using human players to control characters in real time.

Realtime: Happening before your eyes, where the computer can process something as fast as you can view it. The opposite of offline, where the computer requires longer to process something than it takes to view.

Recamming: A machinima technique that allows you to capture the action and then change the camera angle.

Render: To display a 3D model onscreen, starting from the geometry and other physical properties, and resulting in an image.

Scripting: Creating onscreen action by using data.

Server: A computer or computer program that controls a game and keeps all the players in synch.

Skin: A set of textures mapped onto a 3D object to define its appearance. Reskinning involves replacing the original skin with a new skin, so that the object has the same 3D geometry but looks different.

Texture: An image mapped onto a 3D object to define the appearance of its surface.

Viseme: Face shape caused by speech or emotion.

World: The 3D space (or set of 3D spaces) in which a game is played (there are often a certain number of maps within a world).

ACKNOWLEDGMENTS

Special thanks to Hugh Hancock of Strange Company, and also to the many other people who contributed:

Aktrez, **Nabooty Entertainment**
Alexander Jhin, **Society Games**
Anthony Bailey, **Quake Done Quick**
Ashle Kubesh & Kao Lee Thao, **Folklore Studio**
Atussa Simon, **Artemis Software**
Barbara Robertson
Bradford Stephens
Gus and "Burny" Burns, **Rooster Teeth Productions**
Callan McInally, Richard Huddy, & Andrzej Bania, **ATI**
Carrie Cowan, **NVIDIA**
Cat Channon, **Vivendi Universal Games**
Cathy Campos, **Lionhead**
Charles Cecil, **Revolution Software**
Charlie Root, **Mirinae Corporation**
Danielle Peck, Kate Adam, **BBC**
Danny Coffey, **Domasi**
Damien Valentine
David Bancroft, **Electronic Arts**
Denis Cooney, Dave Maiden, & Dave Gildas, **UK Mercs**
Eric "Starfury" Bakutis
Frank Dellario, **The ILL Clan**
Friedrich Kirschner
Ian "Pappy Boyington" Kristensen, **Just Kidding Productions**
Ian Pegler, **Freefilmsoftware.com**
Ian Ruxborough & Shelby Killick, **The Creative Assembly**
Ingrid Moon
Jake Hughes, **Crystal Dynamics**
Jamie Redmond, **OC3 Entertainment**
Jason Choi, **Riot Films**
Jay Lim, **Naontech**
Jeff Morris & Mark Rein, **Epic Games**
Joe Goss, **Tritin Films**
John Brimacombe, **Mforma**
Julia Gastaldi, **Blizzard Entertainment**
Julien Vanhoenacker
Jens "Juliette Sierra" Schöbel

Katherine Anna Kang, **Fountainhead Entertainment**
Katie Olver, **Microsoft**
Ken Thain, **3D Filmmaker**
KOiN and the **Northern Brigade**
Lars Gustavsson, Johan Persson, & Jenny Huldschiner, **Digital Illusions**
Leo Hartas
Leo Lucien-Bay, **Binary Picture Show**
Lidia Stojanovic, **Ubisoft**
Mark Sutherns, **Future Publishing**
Mikko Mononen, **Moppi Productions**
Nathan Moller, **Mu Productions**
Munly Leong
Oliver Bermes, **Dozer Dynamics**
Owain Benallack, **Develop**
Patrick O'Luanaigh, **SCi**
Paul Marino, **Academy of Machinima Arts & Sciences**
Paul Soldera
Paul Weir, **Earcom**
Peter Rasmussen, **Nanoflix Productions**
Richard Gray, **Ritual Entertainment**
Ritesh O'Varma, **Free Monkey**
Robby Huang
Ross Hurrell
Sebastian Tuschy, **Zensen**
Simon Callaghan, **Atari**
Steve Twist
Spoon, and the **Sturmgrenadier Online Gaming Syndicate**
Ted Brown
Tim Ponting, **Activision**
Tom Palmer, **Digital Yolk**
Tony Manninen, **Air Buccaneers Team**
Tony Shiff, **Big Bear Entertainment**
Uwe Girlich
Vincent Scheurer, **Sarrasin LLP**
Xanatos